EAST SIDE STORY

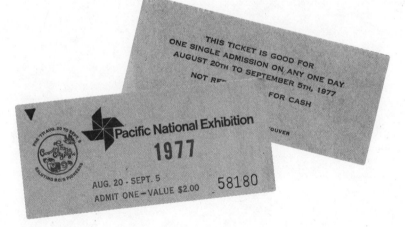

NICK MARINO

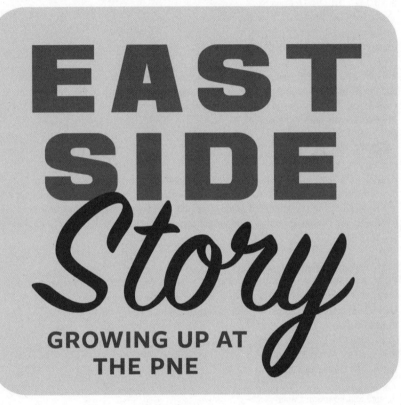

EAST SIDE *Story*

GROWING UP AT
THE PNE

ROBIN'S EGG BOOKS
AN IMPRINT OF
ARSENAL PULP PRESS
VANCOUVER

ROBIN'S EGG BOOKS is an imprint of
ARSENAL PULP PRESS
Suite 202 – 211 East Georgia St.
Vancouver, BC V6A 1Z6
Canada
arsenalpulp.com

The publisher gratefully acknowledges the support of the Canada Council for the Arts
and the British Columbia Arts Council for its publishing program and the Government of
Canada and the Government of British Columbia (through the Book Publishing Tax Credit
Program) for its publishing activities.

Arsenal Pulp Press acknowledges the xʷməθkʷəy̓əm (Musqueam), Sḵwx̱wú7mesh
(Squamish), and səlilwətaɬ (Tsleil-Waututh) Nations, custodians of the traditional, ancestral,
and unceded territories where our office is located. We pay respect to their histories,
traditions, and continuous living cultures and commit to accountability, respectful relations,
and friendship.

Cover and text design by Jazmin Welch
Front cover photograph by Raymond Parker, *Wooden Roller Coaster, Vancouver, 1986*;
back cover photograph courtesy of Nick Marino, his 1984 employee pass
Half title photograph courtesy of Isaac Messinger, a 1977 PNE admission ticket
Edited by Charles Demers
Copy-edited by Catharine Chen
Proofread by Alison Strobel
Indexed by Catharine Chen

Printed and bound in Canada

Library and Archives Canada Cataloguing in Publication:
Title: East Side story : growing up at the PNE / Nick Marino.
Names: Marino, Nick, author.
Description: Includes index.
Identifiers: Canadiana (print) 20230221742 | Canadiana (ebook) 20230222897 |
  ISBN 9781551529332 (softcover) | ISBN 9781551529349 (EPUB)
Subjects: LCSH: Marino, Nick—Childhood and youth. | LCSH: Pacific National Exhibition
  (Vancouver, B.C.) | LCSH: Agricultural exhibitions—British Columbia—Vancouver. |
  LCSH: Fairs—British Columbia—Vancouver. | LCSH: Exhibitions—British Columbia—
  Vancouver. | LCSH: Vancouver (B.C.)—Biography. | LCGFT: Autobiographies.
Classification: LCC S557.C32 V366 2023 | DDC 630.74711/33—dc23

For Jeanne and Dad. Thanks for all the support.

CONTENTS

FOREWORD

In the summer of 2020, in an amusement park running at such reduced capacity as to seem almost abandoned, or else ravaged by some sort of apocalypse (which I guess it had been), my six-year-old daughter and I wore yellow polyester masks of dubious epidemiological efficacy decorated with large cartoon smiles and small Playland logos. This was still early enough in the pandemic that not everyone had really mastered masks yet—in fairness, a significant minority, God bless 'em, never would—and so at one point during the course of the day, I saw another father in an upside-down smile mask, flying through the air on the Sea to Sky Swinger with a look of permanent cartoonish despair.

This all sounds like the makings of a nightmare, and yet our day at Playland was one of the signal mercies of that punishing year. Even without the PNE Fair, without any concerts, without the full offering of rides, and without a guarantee that one wouldn't contract an exotic new disease for which one's body was entirely unprepared (in fairness, that had never been a guarantee the previous years, either), the fact that Playland would open—in any capacity—during that first summer of COVID was the best news we'd heard in months.

That's because the year before, when she'd been five, I had taken my daughter, Joséphine, to PNE/Playland for her very first time and my first in decades. And we each had what we still agree was one of the best days of either of our lives. That day in the summer of 2019, between the endless father-daughter rides and minidonuts and an outdoor Smokey Robinson concert that was a birthday present from my wife—I got to watch the singer I'd listened to as a kid with my mother before she died, performing as though he hadn't grown old

9

right in front of the perfect, sunset-lit North Shore Mountains that would never grow old either—I fell back in love with the PNE.

I had been somewhat disenchanted by the two weeks when I'd worked at the fair in the summer after Grade 10. That was the time I learned that, by some mystery of science, somehow all summer garbage smells the same. For me, sweeping up the food pavilion and sitting next to the trash compactor (not the name of a ride) had robbed the PNE of its romance, but luckily for you readers, none of my friend Nick Marino's many jobs on or around the fairgrounds had the same effect on him.

Helping to prepare this wonderful, touching, and hilarious book—the full up-and-down course of emotions it takes you through might be metaphorically rendered by comparison to, I don't know, some sort of rolling coaster?—I felt an urge to share all of my family's PNE stories. The first house I ever lived in, on Kaslo Street, was less than a five-minute drive from the PNE. I was born a few hours after a Queen concert you will read about in these pages. And, during World War II, in the most ignominious chapter of the fairground's history, my then teenage grandmother went down there to try to find her friend who had been unjustly imprisoned, along with the rest of the city's Japanese Canadian population, as a potential fifth column. Incredibly, she found her friend—who asked her to leave and never come back.

As you will read in the chapters to follow, Vancouverites are dying to share stories of how their individual and family lives join up with the bigger historical life of the city itself at the PNE. Nick has collected their tales—memories that will remind you that before Vancouver discovered Labradoodles and Downward-Facing Dog, it was more like a mangy, uncollared mutt of inscrutable breeding with its snout stuck in a discarded tin of Beefaroni.

But the best guides to East Vancouver by way of the PNE are Nick and his family, the blue-collar descendants of Vancouver's richest

Italian. (True story! Read on.) Nick's dad, Mike, ended his formal education at the age of fifteen, but his tutelage was taken up by his fellow left-wing merchant seamen as he sailed on deep-sea vessels, circumnavigating the globe. Years ago, Nick and I were recording a comedy pilot for CBC Radio, and we needed audio footage of old men complaining about how today's young adults lack the necessary skills of life, from changing tires to basic household repairs. We met up with Mike and his retired longshoremen buddies at a bar at Powell and Victoria in the city's historic East End. We hit "Record," salivating at our chance of getting a tank full of cantankerous. Instead, we got sociological empathy.

"How's your generation supposed to learn any of these skills if you can't afford to buy a home? You can't fix a house you don't have!" Very disappointing from a production standpoint, if heartening from a political one.

Like father, like son: after producing the second draft of the book you now hold in your hands, Nick said to me, "I don't want it to be, like, 'Make East Van Great Again.' A lot of things are way better now. It was super racist. I like a lot of the changes." I know what he means, and yet I also find myself beguiled by the nostalgia.

There is a simultaneous magnetism toward and repulsion from these tales of the extinct East Van. They're stories of a time that was so much tougher, so much more casually violent, and so much less gentle that it's hard to believe it existed within living memory (of those who weren't too badly concussed). In this perhaps overly cautious and hypersanitized era, it's hard not to be a little thrilled in retrospect. One might even say that experiencing the danger of these stories vicariously from a place of safety is something like the packaged exhilaration of, I don't know, a thrill ride in some sort of amusing park.

But it's not nostalgia if it's still happening, and that's the real magic of the PNE. Take any hundred square feet of Playland on any given summer day, and you would be hard pressed to find a greater concentration of racial diversity anywhere on Earth. And yet there is virtually no socioeconomic diversity; the overwhelming majority of people there are working and lower-middle class. It's the kind of place where you might spot, as I have, a grizzled man in shades and matching branded outlaw motorcycle gang T-shirt and sweatpants pushing a baby stroller—and have to resist the urge to scream, "What a little Angel!" PNE/Playland somehow exists as a preserve of the jean jacket Vancouver of my childhood, momentarily pulling the proletarian suburban diaspora back into the town they got Pilates-sculpted out of, if only for a glorious summer day. The fair and its amusement park are among the only civic institutions that belong unequivocally to the popular classes, refusing gentrification like a human body rejecting a bovine heart.

So let Nick Marino, a son of East Vancouver, introduce you to the real PNE. The neighbourhood slogan used to be "Welcome to East Van: Expect No Mercy," but that seems a little dramatic under present circumstances. For now, let's go with "Welcome to East Van: Please Keep Your Arms and Legs Inside the Car for the Duration of the Ride."

Charles Demers
ROBIN'S EGG BOOKS EDITOR

PROLOGUE

The story of the PNE and its place in Vancouver is complex. It has seen the highest highs and the lowest lows in our city. It has been loved, hated, overlooked, underappreciated, and almost forgotten, but it has refused to go away. The PNE of the 1970s and '80s is the backdrop for these stories of the kids who grew up in the shadow of the Wooden Roller Coaster. So, what is the PNE? For most people, it is the two-week fair that takes place at the end of the summer on the sixty hectares (150 acres) of Hastings Park in East Vancouver. The PNE is also the name of the non-profit organization that runs the fair on behalf of the City of Vancouver, the buildings in Hastings Park, and the Playland amusement park. "Hastings Park" and "the PNE grounds" are often used interchangeably, but if we are being technical, the Hastings horse racing track, which is in the park, is not run by the PNE.

But kids from the area didn't care what it was called or who ran it. It was their playground, where they learned to check every door, to hide in the dark, and to sneak through a hole in the fence. It was where they played sports, met their heroes, and held the back door open to let their friends in. For many of them, it was also where they had their first job, their first kiss, and their first drink.

And for a lot of East Van kids, the PNE was home.

The main entrance to the fair, on the corner of Hastings and Renfrew.
CITY OF VANCOUVER ARCHIVES 180-6902.

CHAPTER 1

The Last Summer

IF YOU EVER WORKED AT or went to the fair at the PNE in the early 1980s, you probably saw a massive red-headed teen standing in front of the punching bag machine outside the arcade. A big part of his job was to periodically prove that the machine would actually light up and ring if it was punched hard enough. So, after a series of wannabe tough guys had failed to pass the strongman test, Santino "Red" Scardillo would insert a quarter, drive his giant fist into the bag, and stand stone-faced next to it as the machine flashed and rang out. Sometimes this drummed up customers, but it could also drive them away—especially when he made it ring with a head-butt. To me, Red was as much of a fixture of the PNE in the eighties as Tom Thumb Donuts, the Wooden Roller Coaster, and the demolition derby. That's why I was excited to see him at a retirement party for my brother-in-law, Steve, in 2017.

Red was sitting at a table with Steve, and the years hadn't changed his look all that much. He still had an imposing presence, but his shock of red hair was now considerably shorter. I joined them and let

Red know that I remembered him from when I'd also worked at the PNE. I knew he had been friends with my second cousin, so we had something to talk about. He was happy to be recognized for his time as a bouncer at the arcade and talked nostalgically about the PNE. I've never been much of a risk taker myself and was certainly never a tough guy, but I've always been drawn to characters like Red. I had a sort of risk-adjacent childhood. When I was in Grade 7 and some older kids smoked weed at the park at night, I would join them, but I'd roll up wood chips and lawn clippings and smoke that instead. It made them laugh and allowed me to be part of their world. If they smoked a cigarette, I would eat one. I'm sure they were laughing at me, not with me, but I was just happy to be accepted. I got the same feeling listening to Red's PNE stories. I realized that even though we'd worked at the same place at the same time, we had clearly lived in different worlds.

I started working at the PNE when I was twelve years old, in August 1980. It was two weeks before I started high school and three weeks before I became a teenager. I learned all the necessary skills in my first five minutes on the job. Blow up a balloon, tie it, and replace the popped ones. Blow, tie, replace, repeat. Also, avoid the darts.

The game I worked at was popular with teens because we gave away records as prizes. There weren't any stuffed animals or psyche-delic mirrors to win and trade in for bigger stuffed animals or more garish mirrors. We didn't even have the poster that said "Makin' Bacon" with a picture of two cartoon pigs having sex, which was surprisingly popular. We only had records. For a dollar, the customer was given three darts. If they could pop three balloons in a line, creating a tic-tac-toe, they could spend the rest of the day carrying around a copy of Billy Joel's *Glass Houses* or the soundtrack to *The Blues Brothers*. We had some winners, but most of our customers lost. One guy spent fifty dollars to take home a Pat Benatar record. He was bad at darts but worse with money.

Red Scardillo's employee cards from 1979, 1985, and 1992.
COURTESY OF SANTINO SCARDILLO.

We were told to keep the balloons small, which made them less likely to pop. I've heard that the darts at carnival games are purposely dull to make it hard to pierce the balloons. I'm not sure if that's true, but I know that the darts at our game were sharp enough to pierce my skin. My boss, a sixteen-year-old girl named Susan, was mad when I teased her about a guy, so she threw a dart at me, supposedly to scare me. She threw it a little too hard, however, and it caught me in the forearm that I'd instinctively raised to block it. The game went silent as we all looked at the dart in my arm. It hadn't gone in far enough to cause any real damage, but it did hang there for a few seconds before I pulled it out. Surprisingly, things returned to normal pretty quickly, as if I hadn't just been punctured. The only thing that really changed was that I stopped teasing Susan. The dart in the arm has always been my crazy work story from my years at the PNE in the eighties. Since hearing some of Red's experiences, though, I've told my story a little less.

Red worked throughout the summer at Playland, the amusement park attached to the fair that ran from May to September, as well as working at the fair itself. His first job, at nine years old, was as a ball boy at one of the games. He eventually got a job cleaning up at the arcade and was a bouncer by the time he was sixteen. In the early eighties, there was no actual security at the park, so Red, his teenage co-workers, and the game managers were left to protect the park. He estimates that in his time at the PNE, he was involved in over two hundred fights. That's a lot of fights—Mike Tyson only had a total of eighty-five fights in his amateur and pro careers combined. Red recounts with a chuckle one story that only war veterans or gladiators could relate to in which he witnessed a friend, who also happened to be a sumo wrestler, get hit in the head with a three-foot-long wrench normally used for the rides. The funny part to Red was the fact that his friend was so tough he kept on fighting even though his head had been split open. It's strange to think that these acts of extreme violence took place on the same grounds where, hours earlier, little kids sticky with filth had clutched stuffed animals won by their exhausted parents.

Our game was next to a nearly impossible milk jug / softball toss game run by a horny teenage carny named Pat. He had a stoner's smile, long hair, and a short attention span—unless the topic was girls. He told stories that I wanted to believe of meeting girls at the previous fairs he had worked across Canada. One day, he pulled a dangerous prank in an attempt to impress us. We all watched in horror as Pat used an elastic to slingshot drapery needles at the bunch of helium balloons being carried by an unsuspecting park employee. He missed on his first few attempts, and we winced as the dangerously sharp needles spun through the air like ninja stars, somehow missing the crowd on the midway. When he finally popped one and the vendor looked up at his balloons, confused, Pat laughed like a child who had just heard his first dirty joke. Thankfully, his laughing fit ended the prank and we could relax, knowing no one had lost an eye. He was lucky that Gary, one of the games managers, hadn't seen him.

Gary scared the hell out of me, for a few reasons. The main reason was that he was a grown man who was always enraged. On several occasions, I saw him yelling at workers and patrons, nose to nose like an unhinged baseball manager screaming at an umpire. He had a 1970s undercover cop aesthetic with his curly hair, big moustache, and tinted glasses. My sister, who also worked at the fair, remembers Gary as "imposing, threatening, and kind of buffoonish" and looking "like someone Starsky and Hutch would have arrested." I was surprised that even though he wore a jacket and tie, he often said "cocksucker" and "motherfucker." It's not like I was a stranger to swearing. Elementary school playgrounds are bursting with foul-mouthed kids, but none of the adults I knew swore. Our teachers and coaches never called us "a bunch of lazy cocksuckers," so I wasn't prepared for it when Gary did. I was also scared of him because I was sort of stealing from the game, and I didn't want him to kill me.

I didn't handle any money as my job was just to blow, tie, and replace balloons. But I noticed that the teenage bosses would on occasion slip a twenty-dollar bill into their back pocket. It's inevitable that if you pay a teenager $3.40 an hour and then tie an apron full of money around their waist, there is going to be some financial leakage. I'm not saying it's right, just that it's inevitable. Over the six summers I worked there, it seemed that every employee, at every level, was taking something. I assume that some people weren't scamming—I just never met them.

I'd never intended to take money from the fair, but when the opportunity presented itself, I didn't run away from it. I was the first one at the game one morning and was standing behind the counter when a pockmarked teen wearing a PNE food services shirt sauntered up and suggested a simple deal. If I gave him free records, he would give me free food from the concession stand. The idea of an endless supply of junk food was irresistible, and within a couple of minutes of our meeting, he was walking away with a copy of Supertramp's *Breakfast in America,* and I was dreaming of onion rings and cheeseburgers. When I got my free food that day, I gave him five dollars as part of the charade of a real transaction. I was surprised and pretty excited when, instead of giving me the five dollars back in change, he gave me twenty-seven. I filled my pocket with the stolen money, anxiously looked around for Gary, and planned on arriving early again the next day.

While I was becoming a preteen criminal, Red was working the arcade and keeping the park safe from "heatbaggers." There is a 1982 *Vancouver Sun* article about the PNE in which the writer tries to learn the meaning of *heatbagger,* a specifically East Vancouver word. In it, Red is quoted as saying a heatbagger is a "guy who likes to cause trouble. Knock over garbage cans. Pinch girls' bums. Stuff like that."[1]

The concession stand where I got free food in exchange for records.
CITY OF VANCOUVER ARCHIVES 180-6572.

It was a sign of the times that littering and sexual assault were seen as equal offences. The presence of Red and some of the other giant bouncers was often enough to keep things calm, but the bouncers had their fair share of tussles removing heatbaggers from the park. You don't get into two hundred fights by turning the other cheek. Red claims that after that article was published, guys would come to the fair just to challenge him to a fight.

Because he worked from 11:00 a.m. to closing time every day for the seventeen days of the fair, Red ended up living there. He stayed in a room above the arcade with a fellow bouncer. At the end of each shift, they would clean the floors, wipe down the machines, and secure the money before inviting friends to join them for late-night parties. Often, they had barbecues, played the arcade games for free, and drank while listening to the Cars on an eight-track. They were like kids in a candy store, except they were teens with alcohol in a free arcade, which is infinitely better. It was the experience of going to battle together, celebrating together, and being entrusted with the security of the park that made his co-workers feel like a family to Red. His job was important, and he was a visible and respected member of the park. In contrast, I was a twelve-year-old boy who blew up balloons and dodged darts. Like many kids in their first job, I was basically invisible, which was fine with me as long as Gary didn't see me handing out records.

I ended up swapping records for burgers a few more times and was lucky to never get caught. It was the most exciting part of my first year at the PNE. Actually, it was the second most exciting thing, because on one of the last days of the fair, some high school girls from the suburbs with feathered hair and flared jeans were playing our game and asked me and the other balloon blower, Dave, if we wanted to hang out when our shift ended.

When the girls arrived at our game at 5:00 p.m., we jumped over the counter, excited for our group "date." I had a little extra pocket money, having unloaded a copy of *Eat to the Beat* by Blondie that morning, so I was happy to play lots of games and share some minidonuts. We never held their hands or kissed them, but walking through the park with those four high school girls from the Valley, cracking jokes and watching them laugh with each other, is one of the most vivid memories of that summer. I knew that my parents had expected me home hours earlier, but I couldn't just leave. At about eight o'clock, we ended up back at our game.

Pat, who seemed to work twelve hours a day, called us over so he could flirt with the girls. His game was so difficult that the only prizes were giant stuffed animals. No trading up was required, as nobody could possibly win twice. As the girls stood around looking at the oversized plush prizes, Pat passed me a softball to try the game for free. Over the last couple of weeks, I had seen hundreds of people aim at the large metal milk jug, only to see their balls bounce off the rim of the container. I suspected the hole wasn't even big enough to fit a softball. Still, I gripped the ball and threw it with some backspin. Somehow, it fell silently and perfectly into the milk jug. It was incredible. No one ever won at Pat's game. The girls cheered and started pointing at the prizes they wanted. I was the king of the fair. Then Pat laughed and said, "Sorry, buddy, that was just practice. You gotta pay to win." We pleaded for the prize, offered to pay, but Pat would not relent. Eventually, I had to leave, as it was getting dark and I was way past due at home. I said goodbye, and the girls faded into the crowd, still with Dave. I could hear them laughing as I headed off into the warm summer night, feeling a little more grown up than my twelve years.

Soon I would be home, fabricating reasons for being late, while back at the PNE, Red and his buddies would just be getting started. After completing all the shutdown activities around midnight, they would start their arcade party. These parties often included other workers from the park, which opened up more opportunities for fun. If an operator from the roller coaster was with them, they might be given free rides in the dark. Sometimes they would stay on the ride for twenty or thirty trips in a row. Eventually, as they searched for new thrills, the guys found a way to raise the stakes. A lot. They dared each other to switch seats during the ride.

The Coaster was built in 1958 and is currently ranked as the seventh best wooden roller coaster in the world, according to a poll by *ElloCoaster*, an online thrill-seekers publication.[2] The ride is anything but smooth, as every turn and drop threatens to throw you out of your seat. There are no seat belts or shoulder harnesses. The only thing keeping you from flying out is a metal bar that is pulled down across your lap and locked in place by the ride attendant. Red and his friends soon figured out a way to keep the lap bar from locking, which allowed them to frantically switch seats with the person next to them while the train car was going up a hill. Red claims it escalated to swapping seats with the people behind or in front of them while the ride was in progress. They were clearly taking their lives into their own hands, riding without any safety restraints at speeds up to nearly eighty kilometres an hour (fifty miles per hour) and at heights equal to a seven-storey building. For ninety seconds, as they rocketed through twists, turns, and camel hops, the guys who spent their days protecting the park lived on the edge of disaster. At times, they would have to pull each other back into the seats as gravity tried to pull them out. Mostly, they howled and laugh as they careened around the track, ignoring both the laws of physics and common sense.

My last day of work that summer was on Labour Day, which was also the day before I started high school. The seventeen days of the fair had been a great warm-up for Grade 8. I had broken the law, watched adults scream at each other, and spent time with actual teenage girls. I couldn't have asked for more. Things would change quickly, however, not just for me, but also for the PNE. Within a year, my mom would die, my grades would plummet, and I would start drinking. The summer of 1980 was truly the last summer of my childhood. As for the PNE, it would continue but soon become relegated to the status of a regional fair, as in November the city was awarded the 1986 World's Fair.

Vancouver would use Expo 86 as a sort of fake ID to get into the club of "world-class cities." The pull of the west side of the city would eventually take Vancouver's three pro sports teams away from the PNE grounds too. The upwardly mobile version of Vancouver that grew from the seeds of Expo 86 would always be at odds with the blue-collar East Side aesthetic of the PNE. Characters like Red, Pat, and Gary didn't exist within the corporate structures that overtook the city's sports and entertainment industries. Vancouver was on a mission to be a world-class city, and in doing so, turned its back on the history and character of places like the PNE. In 1980, Vancouver was a lot like me: small, overconfident, and way too excited about growing up.

CHAPTER 2

Free Ride!

ON SEPTEMBER 9, 1968, from all over Vancouver people can see light rising from the highest point of the Wooden Roller Coaster at the PNE. It isn't coming from searchlights or fireworks, however. This time, the Wooden Roller Coaster is on fire, and flames are shooting ninety metres (three hundred feet) up into the air. A group of fourteen-year-old boys were lighting fires in the trash cans between the concessions and the roller coaster. Things quickly got out of hand, the boys fled, and the fire spread, wrapping around a strip of concessions before grabbing hold of the coaster.

People gather on the grounds and outside the fence to watch the blaze. Forty-five firefighters, hampered by locked gates and a lack of hydrants, work to douse the flames. After an hour, the fire is brought under control. The boys have escaped, but not without being seen. Descriptions of a youth gang wearing white T-shirts with skull insignias are passed to the press and the police. For now, they are free, but that might not last. Fifteen concession stands have been completely flattened by the fire, and the roller coaster is out of commission indefinitely.

A month later, five of the boys find themselves in court, charged with arson. As they are only fourteen years old, their names are not published, but the local kids know who they are. The boys plead not guilty. And they wait. For three months they don't know whether they will spend the next few years locked up or roaming the streets. Then, on December 30, 1968, the charges are dropped due to "lack of evidence."[3] What started out as front-page news a few months earlier ends up a two-sentence story on the last page of the paper. The Coaster is not ready for operation until seven months after the fire. The estimated damage: $300,000.

The Coaster had been standing for only ten years when the boys lit the fire. It was the third in a line of giant wooden roller coasters in Vancouver. In the early days of the fair, the most thrilling ride at the park was the Dip the Dips coaster, also known as Leap the Dips, until it was replaced by the Giant Dipper in 1925. The Giant Dipper was a rollicking beast that threw patrons around in their seats with jolts and twists so severe that a book about the PNE claims it was "so terrifying that local myth suggests it was a fairly reliable abortifacient."[4] The

The Giant Dipper, postcard from the 1920s.
CITY OF VANCOUVER ARCHIVES AM1052 P-2151.

Giant Dipper also received a bizarre testimonial in a 1928 issue of the *Vancouver Daily Province*. In a promotional story, a fictional explorer claims, "I have shot lions and golfed in Scotland, but never in my life had a thrill to compare with that given me when I first rode the Giant Dipper at Happyland."[5] And the ride wasn't just for pregnant teens and trophy hunters—the general public loved it too.

In 1948 the Giant Dipper was demolished to make way for a racetrack, and the city was without a major roller coaster for ten years. The new Wooden Roller Coaster unveiled in 1958 is the same one that stands today. According to *The Province* newspaper, it was the fastest and highest roller coaster in North America at the time. Three hundred workers, including a team of Norwegian shipbuilders, worked on the ride, which ended up costing $200,000. (I'm not exactly sure how you do $300,000 worth of damage to a $200,000 structure, but that's how badass those little arsonists were, I guess.) For a time, it was also referred to as the Giant Dipper, but now it is known simply as the Coaster.

It is loud, rickety, scary, and everything you want from a roller coaster. It has also been remarkably safe. The only incidents that have ever happened on it were the result of poor choices by the riders, like this one, described in a 1985 article in the *Vancouver Sun*:

> Several years ago, they found pieces of one yahoo who tried changing his seat while the coaster was entering the straightaway. The fellow flew off and busted a board with his head. He lived but was permanently injured. [The Coaster foreman] occasionally sees him drinking at the Lougheed Hotel ... The crew mounted the bloodied board on a wall of their workshop.[6]

It's hard to believe that the Coaster has lasted so long. As of this writing, it is sixty-five years old. I remember looking at it when I worked there in the 1980s and thinking back then that it was old.

In 1983, the man who had overseen the roller coaster for two decades said, "She's good for another ten or fifteen years."[7] That would have spelled its retirement by 1998 at the latest. And, for a while, that was the plan.

In 1996, Vancouver City Council unanimously voted in favour of reverting Hastings Park to green space. A Vancouver city document from that year entitled *The Greening of Hastings Park* states that "the PNE and Playland will both cease to operate in Hastings Park."[8] Although some buildings were planned to be preserved, all the concessions and rides, including the Coaster, were slated for demolition. The document also suggests that the new park "should examine a variety of ways in which the site history might be recorded into the fabric of the park."[9] This included using parts of the deconstructed roller coaster as a garden sculpture in the new green space. However, city plans changed, and Playland and the PNE remain a part of Hastings Park to this day. The city declared the Coaster a site of special significance in 2008, fifty years after it first opened. It was commemorated with a plaque reading:

> Once threatened with demolition, the 1958 Wooden Roller Coaster is celebrated across North America as the last, still operating example of noted designer Carl Phare's work. Built of Douglas Fir by Walker LeRoy, the coaster features a maximum drop height of 20m and speeds of up to 76km/h. As Canada's oldest operating wooden roller coaster, it is designated as a "Coaster Landmark," and a "Coaster Classic" by the American Coaster Enthusiasts organization.

In a decade, the Coaster went from being condemned to being protected. So much for the levelling of the rides and concessions—it seems that the PNE and Playland are here to stay. And I think most people do agree that the Wooden Roller Coaster is a site of special

The Coaster in 1959, when it was only a year old.
CITY OF VANCOUVER ARCHIVES 180-3482.

significance in Vancouver. It provides the soundtrack and backdrop to the fair. Wherever you are on the midway, you can hear the train cars rumble and shake while the riders shriek and howl. Even the *tick, tick, tick* sound it makes going up the first hill is enough to make me feel anxious when I am just walking past. Visually, the colossal structure anchors the park. Its sheer size dares parkgoers to either conquer it or avoid it. Either way, you have to respect it. It is the king of the park. Also, of all the rides at in the park, the Coaster is by far the coolest one to work at.

I asked Eric, a friend of mine from high school who worked at the Coaster in the mid-1980s, to explain a typical day working the fair's most popular ride. He claims that he started each day by having sex with a girl from the petting zoo in his van, parked behind the roller coaster. That's significantly different from how I started my day at the darts game, which was a lot more balloon centred. After the girl left to spend the rest of her day feeding pigs and sweeping up goat shit, Eric would start work. He walked the entirety of the track with a manager, looking for any bolts that needed tightening or plates that may have popped up and doing a visual inspection of the brakes, though the more mechanical tasks were handled by the managers rather than the seasonal guys like Eric. Once everything looked safe, they gave it a couple of trial runs. Eric says there were always some girls who wanted to ride for free in the morning, so he would let them on for the test rides. If everything looked good to the operators, the ride would open. Then it was just the routine of slowing and stopping the trains with the brake levers, unlocking the safety bars, locking the new riders into their seats, and letting the train go.

The only times things got a bit dicey was when the operators waited too long to slow down a train before it reached the platform.

Eric taking a break at the Coaster in the 1980s.
COURTESY OF ERIC KOPROWSKI.

Eric says sometimes he would be "talking to some chicks or changing the station on the radio" and the train would be coming in too fast. Even after they applied the brakes, the train would stop past the platform, and it would "look stupid." So instead of letting themselves look bad, the guys would yell, "KEEP YOUR HANDS IN! FREE RIDE! FREE RIDE!" and let the passengers take another lap. During the fair, there were often three trains going at once on the track. They weren't on any sort of mechanical timer, though. Instead, the operators just estimated when to let each train go. It was the managers deciding to run things this way, leaving guys like Eric to fasten safety bars and think of ways to scam a bit more money.

Eric had a few ways to supplement his income. Since he parked his van behind the roller coaster, he had a key for one of the gates. He used this to let in friends for free and other people for half price. He also sold stolen ride tickets for 50 percent off, which he referred to as "the full meal deal" in reference to a promotion at Dairy Queen at the time. Now, he laughs about his brazen transactions and claims it was what everyone else was doing to some degree, anyway. Eric tells me that ride managers would get bonuses based on the number of tickets sold. The tickets were not tracked or counted, however, as this was way before computers were used at the park. Instead, the used tickets were weighed each day, and Eric claims that he saw managers wetting their tickets before getting them weighed.

Eric isn't really sure why he was chosen to work at the roller coaster. He is proud of the fact that he worked the premium ride and suspects he was there for security. At nineteen, Eric was a pretty intimidating guy. He says, "Yeah, I don't know what they saw in me. You know, maybe they just needed somebody to punch people out if they got out of control or whatever." It never really came to that, but his presence probably had a calming effect on any would-be tough guys the same way Red's presence discouraged people from acting up at the arcade. Eventually, many years later, Eric and Red would work together as part of the park's security at various events, including raves and concerts.

The roller coaster was also a meeting place for after-hours parties. Vanessa, a friend of mine who worked at food concessions and midway games, remembers parties of up to thirty local teens and travelling carnies underneath the shadow of the Coaster. When a group of school friends wanted a place to meet up for drinks, the roller coaster was a natural choice. It's not like teens are going to want to hang out by the kiddie helicopters or the merry-go-round. Throw in a few of the unpredictable carnies who worked throughout the midway, and it was a pretty good night. The mornings could be a little hard, however. Vanessa was surprised one morning when she opened her game, and a hungover carny rolled out from under the counter after spending the night passed out on top of the stuffed animal prizes.

It wasn't just carnies who travelled from out of town to the PNE. The PNE was just another stop on the fair circuit for many entertainers and publicity seekers from other cities. In 1979, twenty-one-year-old Richard Rodriguez from Brooklyn, New York, came to town to break the Guinness World Record for longest continuous ride on a roller coaster. The plan was to ride for 170 consecutive hours, which is one week and two hours. He was allowed a five-minute break per hour to go to the washroom and quickly eat some food. He would lie on the floor of the roller coaster car to sleep, though I'm not sure how that was possible. His eighteen-year-old business agent claimed that Rodriguez was "not likely to have an arm or foot sticking out while he sleeps." Seven days and 3,310 trips around the track later, Rodriguez emerged from his car and drank a glass of champagne, which he somehow didn't throw up. For a little while, the old Wooden Roller Coaster was part of *The Guinness Book of World Records*.

I remember hearing in the mid-1980s that my friend Travis had ridden the roller coaster for the duration of the fair while wearing a local radio station's mascot costume. However, after giving him a call, I learned that I had misremembered what actually happened. He didn't ride the roller coaster at all—it was the Ferris wheel. And it wasn't just him. There were three guys sharing two costumes. They took turns riding the giant wheel in their hellishly hot costumes, from opening to closing. After a shift, the costume would be dripping with sweat, so they would turn it inside out as much as possible in hopes it would dry out a bit before the next guy had to put it on. Then they'd find a spot to smoke weed until it was their turn to ride again.

Travis claims that riding the Ferris wheel in a mascot costume was not only crazy hot, but also very stressful. There were always people who wanted to ride with the mascot, and because the suit was so awkward and the guys were always stoned, they'd worry about accidentally knocking someone off the top of the wheel and then having their mascot head pulled off by an angry mob to reveal their bloodshot eyes before being dragged away by the police. They could have avoided this situation by not always being high, but that didn't seem to be an option.

I'd called Travis hoping to hear a story about a guy in a mascot costume getting tossed around on the roller coaster for twelve hours a day. Instead, I got the story of three stoners sharing two sweaty costumes and worrying about getting arrested for manslaughter.

CHAPTER 3

The Gayway

BY THE LATE 1970S, the Pacific National Exhibition was falling out of favour in Vancouver. People still attended but brought the level of enthusiasm usually reserved for family dinners. It might be fun, but it will also be predictable and probably give you a stomach ache. A *Vancouver Sun* article in 1977 opens with "It's corny, it's hick, it's awful ..."[10] A 1980 *Province* column proclaims, "Like most people, I say I hate the PNE. Like most people, I will probably go again this year."[11] These pieces usually ended with a "he's a chump, but he's *our* chump" sort of sentiment and a resignation that the PNE was here to stay. Even Erwin Swangard, president of the PNE, agreed that the fair was getting "boring."[12] But how did the PNE, which was once the second-largest fair of its kind in North America, become something that the public only grudgingly supported?

The affordability of air travel certainly had something to do with it. As planes became larger in the seventies, airlines were able to sell more tickets at cheaper prices, making flights affordable for middle-class families. A common destination was California, specifically Disneyland. Once people saw the Magic Kingdom, it was impossible for them not to compare it to the travelling carny show that the PNE resembled. Newspaper articles about the PNE in the 1950s and

'60s are generally positive. By the 1970s, however, the tone changes, and the fair is often presented as outdated, which is inevitable for something based on a model developed in the previous century. As people saw more of the outside world, there was a feeling that the PNE needed to change with the times.

To really understand how the PNE became less exciting for many Vancouverites in the 1970s, it's important to look at what the fair was like in the decades leading up to its decline. And to be honest, it seemed a little "corny and hick" even then. Take, for example, a story from the *Vancouver Sun* on August 29, 1950. The headline reads, "Thief Grabs $80 from PNE Show." The article covered three bizarre incidents at the fair from the same day: the headlining robber using a cob of corn to his advantage; a child taking a sledgehammer to the skull; and a woman getting run over by a train. The story of the stolen eighty dollars feels particularly small town. A teenage girl named Betty was working as a cashier outside the snake show. After collecting the money and securing it in a cigar box, she decided to eat a corn on the cob, which is an odd choice of snack if your job is handling money. The thief must have thought the same as he watched and waited. As soon as Betty put both of her hands on her buttery cob, he pounced, grabbing the cigar box and running away. Betty chased the thief but was unable to recover the money. The suspect, an eighteen-year-old who had been spotted loitering on the midway, was not caught. I assume he roamed the grounds looking for another hungry cashier about to dig into a plate of crab legs or cherries jubilee.

The other incidents continue this B-movie feeling. At the strong-man game, a boy was struck in the head with a fifteen-pound sledgehammer while trying to get a better view; he required medical treatment. You'd think the whole sledgehammer to a child's skull story would trump the corncob robbery for headline space, but this anecdote was buried near the end of the article. Meanwhile, that same day, the miniature train conductor in Kiddieland had spotted a group of women walking on the track, tooted his horn, and tried to stop. The women scattered, but one of them fell in front of the train and was run over, suffering a "lacerated left leg and possible fracture of her left foot." Scores of kids witnessed the accident, as it was Children's Day, one of the busiest days of the fair. It's hard to imagine any of these three incidents ever happening at a modern theme park. In 1950, however, they all happened on the same day and were noted only in a small article at the back of the newspaper.

That dangerous 1950 Children's Day does line up with a lot of the stories my dad has told me about growing up in East Vancouver in the 1940s and '50s. There was a general lack of supervision back then; groups of elementary school–aged kids routinely wandered the streets. Most of them smoked, and my dad remembers going with

The train that ran over a woman on Children's Day in 1950.
CITY OF VANCOUVER ARCHIVES 180-3893.

friends to a corner store near the PNE to buy single cigarettes from a man known as Vic the Gyp, an inappropriate nickname by today's standards for a man engaged in business practices also inappropriate by today's standards. Vic sold the boys loose cigarettes for a nickel. They were often unsatisfied, however, as the tightly rolled English cigarettes Vic sold to kids were difficult to "get a good pull out of" with their ten-year-old lungs.

My dad and his friends had seen Bull Durham brand tobacco in the movies and wanted to try it, but it wasn't available in Canada. So, one day, they decided to ride their bikes from East Vancouver to Blaine, Washington, to try to find some. ("When I was a kid, we had to ride our bikes to another country to get premium tobacco!") My dad, who was twelve years old at the time, his older brother Nick, and a few friends set off on their adventure with no more than their bikes and some money for tobacco. The return trip would be over a hundred kilometres (sixty miles) on their fixed gear bikes, with no backup inner tubes or water bottles.

They had to cross the border. I'm not sure what they planned to say in response to the border guard's question, "What is the purpose of your trip?" They didn't have any documentation or letters of permission from their parents—just a curiosity to try the same tobacco they had seen in movies. In any case, they were waved through. They bought some American chocolate bars and Bull Durham tobacco from a corner store, then rolled up some cigarettes and explored the small border town on their bikes while smoking. As the sun began to set, they realized that the route would be difficult to make out in the dark, so they decided to spend the night in Blaine. An abandoned car near a vacant lot seemed like a good place to sleep, until they disturbed a nest of rats and one of the kids got bitten. They piled out of the car and slept outside. When the sun rose, they got back on their bikes and crossed the border with their pockets full of Bull Durham tobacco.

My dad playing violin and possibly thinking about buying cigarettes.
COURTESY OF MIKE MARINO.

Stories like this help put into perspective some of the newspaper articles I've read about the PNE's past. For example, one article from August 1957 tells of a runaway kid whose adventure reminds me of my dad's cross-border tobacco trip. Eleven-year-old Louis from New Westminster was excited to go to the PNE with his parents. They promised to take him to the fair in a week, but Louis couldn't bear to wait, so he ran away from home. He left his house at 9:00 a.m. and wasn't seen or heard from by his parents again until noon the next day. Bringing the two dollars he had earned as a reward for finding a lost cat, he went to the fair on his own and had a great time, keeping his expenses down by filling up on food samples. As night fell, he realized it was too late to make it home, so he decided to sleep in an empty horse stable. Some stablemen saw Louis lying in a bed of hay but decided it wasn't worth telling anyone. After all, it was just an unsupervised eleven-year-old in a stable at midnight.

Louis rose early the next day ("Those horses sure wake you up") and carried on with his adventure.[13] He still had fifty cents, so he went on some rides, checked out the machine guns at a military display, and tried his luck at the casino, winning a quarter. I'm sure kids weren't technically allowed to gamble at the PNE, but the article just states matter-of-factly that Louis, an eleven-year-old, won money at the casino. When he finally ran out of cash, he borrowed a dime from a woman and called home to get picked up by his dad. The article claims he was taken home for a good night's sleep and a talking to. I'm not sure if this was 1950s code for a beating by his parents, so I will hope that Louis went to sleep unharmed.

Like many kids in East Vancouver, my dad worked at the PNE. In 1947, when he was twelve years old, he had a job slicing buns at a hamburger stand. He sat in the front, where everyone could see him cutting the buns in half and putting them into a bucket. He was told that if he happened to drop one on the sawdust-covered ground, he should put the dirty bun into a separate bucket, as a public display of trust. Then he would take both the bucket of clean buns and the bucket of dirty buns to the back of the stand, out of the customers' view, and dump them both into the same container. These would be piled with fried onions and a grilled beef patty and sold with a smile out front.

He also had a variety of jobs that no longer exist in Vancouver. When he was eleven, he worked as a shoeshine boy until, in the middle of a job and after eating too much roast pork and applesauce, he threw up down the stairs of an illegal bookie joint. At thirteen, he got a job salting the streetcar tracks in Gastown; he would be dropped off alone in the middle of the night with a shovel and a load of salt. He spent time as a paper shuffler at the *Vancouver Sun*, manually stuffing sections of the newspaper together in a room full of newsprint and smoking teenagers. At fourteen, he lied his way into a job as a whistle punk, which put him alone in the middle of a forest, sending signals through a long wire to ensure the safety of a logging operation. He left home at the age of fifteen and worked as a mess boy on a ship to England. By the time I was fifteen, I had only ever worked at the PNE, blowing up balloons and handing out bingo cards.

My dad, Mike Marino (right), with a friend in the early 1950s.
COURTESY OF MIKE MARINO.

Even though it was easy to find a variety of jobs in postwar Vancouver, many East Vancouver teens ended up working at the PNE, a job that would end seventeen days after it started. It was the summer romance of jobs, with no long-term commitments or actual loyalty required. One of the main areas of employment for young people was the midway, or as it was called back then, the Gayway. The midway is generally the busiest part of a fair and includes the games, rides, food, and entertainment. It is separate from the exhibition halls and agricultural buildings. The Gayway of the midcentury PNE had carnival games, the Big Dipper, gambling tents, a stripper tent, the Monkey Drome, a "freak show," and more. If you were willing to overlook rampant exploitation, there was a lot of fun to be had on the Gayway.

There is a common misconception that fairs like the PNE are dishonest, that they are trying to unfairly separate you from your money. But all businesses are trying to get your money. At least with a fair, you know their intentions from the second you walk in the gate. In fact, an article from August of 1951 claims that the midway at the PNE "tops Canada for honesty."[14] That same article also mentions how one of the gambling tents on the Gayway was shut down for cheating patrons out of the biggest prizes, so in this case, honesty is relative. Occasionally, the travelling carnies who operated the sideshows, games, and attractions would have a problem with the rules put in place by the PNE and the watchful eye of the Vancouver Police. In the 1950s, bets at the gambling tents were capped at twenty-five cents, but police claimed that some operators were accepting wagers as high as fifty dollars. The carnival chief ordered four booths to shut down after hearing about these violations. A protest against these closures was quickly organized, and the entire Gayway was shut down by a sit-down protest that shuttered over forty games, fifteen sideshows, and seven rides. Even Lorina, Queen of the Nudists, joined the protest with complaints of her own, including the PNE's failure to provide lights, a platform, and a box office. Unironically, the nudist queen angrily claimed that she was "losing her shirt."[15] The freak show operators also joined the protest. I'm not sure if having the freak show guys on your side is morally a good thing, but it was an impressive display of solidarity.

The operators from out of town seemed to bring a sense of vigilante justice with them. As lifelong carnies, they were willing to take situations into their own hands. On a night in 1957 at the fair, Edward Perry, the freak show operator, had to fend off three "thugs" in the middle of a show.[16] (*Thug* is a very common word in 1950s articles

A crowd on the Gayway in 1950.
CITY OF VANCOUVER ARCHIVES 180-5075.

about criminals.) The thugs were caught trying to sneak under the canvas tent into the show and were thrown out by Perry. The men returned to the tent with a knife, a lead pipe, and a nickel-plated automatic pistol to take revenge, though it also sounds like they were ready for a live action recreation of the board game Clue. They forced their way through the crowd, spotted Perry, and the man holding the pistol fired a shot at him. Perry dodged the bullet and responded by throwing a sledgehammer at the trio, hitting the knife-wielding man in the back. They fled the scene, and Perry was able to refocus his energy on monetizing his "freaks."

In the late 1970s, twenty years after the freak show shooting, the PNE hadn't really changed that much, but the world had. Vancouverites had travelled and begun expecting more from their city. The PNE had become stagnant, a thing of the past. Anyone under seventy-five probably couldn't remember a time when the PNE didn't exist. And, as familiarity breeds contempt, there was a desire for the city to take the next step, to reinvent itself. Not content to be a working-class western outpost, a younger sibling to Canada's larger eastern cities, Vancouver looked to rebrand itself. Perhaps it was the outdated carny feel of the midway or the fact that it really hadn't changed with the times, but something made people believe that the city had outgrown the PNE, the same way one might feel when returning to an old neighbourhood. In time, however, the PNE would prove to be much more resilient than anyone expected, because the people who loved it the most, the kids, were never the ones who complained. It's the kids and teens that keep the PNE alive. They may not be sleeping overnight in horse barns or betting at the casino anymore, but they bring a level of enthusiasm that most adults can't muster. They loved the fair just as it was the last time they went, and all they want is for it to be the same when they come back.

And, trust me, it will.

The Pacific Coliseum in the 1970s.
CITY OF VANCOUVER ARCHIVES 180-3623.

CHAPTER 4

How to Sneak Into the Coliseum

(AND HOW TO GET THROWN OUT)

AT TWELVE YEARS OLD, I wanted nothing more than to be in high school. I would spend hours at home flipping through my brother Mike's yearbook, thinking about how exciting it was going to be when I finally got there. Mike is four years older than me, and until I was ten we shared a room, where we'd often be in tears from laughing so hard when we were supposed to be asleep. I would go to watch every basketball game he played at Killarney Secondary School in East Vancouver and all his away games throughout the city. I'd come home and practise shooting hoops at my elementary school, hoping to one day be like him. Then, to make my mom laugh, I would recreate the cheerleader's halftime dance. To be honest, I enjoyed getting the laughs from my mom more than playing basketball.

As well as looking up to my brother, I was also in awe of my cousins, Ed and Mike (or Mikey), who were six and eight years older than me. They let me hang out with their friends when I visited.

I didn't say much, but I took in their stories of crazy teammates, girls, and general overindulgence. I made a mental note of their antics and assumed I would eventually live the same life. At the time, I didn't realize that my brother and cousins were all much bigger risk takers than me. I loved to hear their stories, but I preferred to be next to chaos than in the centre of it. There was always a part of me that worried about getting hurt or in trouble. Even though I shared DNA with these guys, taking risks was somehow not in mine. Over the years, foolishly looking at their lives as the blueprint for mine, I made several poor decisions.

In much the same way that I looked to my brother and cousins for direction, Vancouver in the 1960s looked to Toronto and Montreal, two major metropolitan cities with teams in the National Hockey League. When the NHL decided to expand in 1967, Vancouverites assumed that their city would be included. Instead, six American teams were added to the league. Vancouver's first step to becoming a world-class city was a stumble. At one point, the owners of the Toronto Maple Leafs were behind a bid to get Vancouver a team in the NHL. They wanted the city to give them prime downtown land for a new arena, but instead, the city offered a ninety-nine-year lease for a dollar per year. The Maple Leafs owners balked at this offer. Then, on a civic ballot in 1964, Vancouver voters said no on a plebiscite that would have seen the land given away for free and an arena built at the current location of the downtown library and the CBC. This opened the door for the PNE to pitch Hastings Park, on the east side of the city, as an alternate site for the arena. The city agreed, and the Pacific Coliseum was opened on the PNE grounds on January 8, 1968, at a cost of $6 million. The intention was to lure the NHL to the city. It didn't work at first, but by 1970, Vancouver become the proud home of one of the worst teams in professional sports: the Canucks. Meanwhile, scores of East Side kids started working on schemes to get into the brand-new arena without paying.

The Pacific Coliseum, situated on the west side of the PNE grounds, was not built just to house the Canucks. Over the years, it has hosted countless amazing shows and sporting events. In the 1980s alone, I saw David Bowie film his *Serious Moonlight* concert video, watched Prince work the audience with endless energy, shouted "BRUUUUUUUUCE!" at Springsteen from the second row, and jumped onstage with the Clash. I watched Marvin Hagler knock out Thomas Hearns on a satellite broadcast in one of the most exciting sporting events I've ever seen. But none of these events even came close to the excitement I felt as an eight-year-old watching the preshow entertainment on August 31, 1976.

Our family was at the Coliseum to see the double bill of comedian John Byner and singer Della Reese—part of the PNE Star Spectacular concert series. My family loved John Byner from his regular appearances on variety and talk shows in the 1970s. He went on to create *Bizarre*, a sketch show that was filmed in Canada and featured Super Dave Osborne. Della Reese was a jazz singer from the 1950s and '60s whom my mom had followed since her teens. I don't remember much from either of their performances, aside from the fact that I laughed a lot at Byner and that Reese sang a song from *The Wiz*. What I will always remember, however, was watching a guy running from security before the show started.

These were the days before any officially sanctioned preshow entertainment or cellphones, when families had no choice but to talk to each other or stare blankly around the arena. The arena was half-full when the audience, who had probably run out of things to say, quickly spotted and cheered on a young man eluding security. He ran down the stairs in a section opposite the stage with two security "guards" in pursuit. I have to put *guards* in quotation marks because these guys were really just ushers in blue-polyester PNE blazers, middle-aged men with average athletic prowess, at best. The audience cheered each time the perp broke free of the ushers. He ran in and out of sections, sometimes disappearing only to be spotted a few sections over, prompting more cheers from the crowd. Watching this all unfold as an eight-year-old was awesome. I loved when adults looked silly, and the ushers were looking pretty inept. If we had gone home after this chase ended, it would have been enough for me. My brother, sister, and I laughed and cheered. Then things suddenly became exponentially more exciting—and personal.

As my mom, the most reasonable member of our family, watched the distraction along with the rest of us, a realization came to her, one that made the whole situation almost mind blowing for me. "Jesus Christ," she said, "is that Mikey?" And lucky for us, it was indeed my seventeen-year-old cousin who was putting on this show. We cheered even louder as Mikey continued to dodge the ushers. He got closer and managed to blend into the audience in the folding seats at the front of the stage, just a few rows from us. My mom made eye contact and called him over. "Auntie Diane!" he said, before taking a seat in the row behind us. He immediately took off his jacket to avoid being recognized. My mom seemed nervous for him but not mad. I just stared at him, full of pride. My cousin was the guy we were all cheering for, the guy who brought us together as an audience.

Mikey seemed relaxed, considering he was being pursued in front of thousands of people. After a couple of minutes and some rushed small talk, a few ushers spotted him and began descending on the floor. Mikey sensed it was time to go, grabbed his jacket, and slunk off. He started in a fast walk with his head down, but quickly got back into a sprint, with the ushers on his heels. At one point, one of them threw a flashlight at him. It missed and smashed against the cement wall of the concourse. The crowd cheered as Mikey continued to evade capture. Eventually though, he was boxed in by four ushers, two coming down the stairs of one section while the other two pursued from behind. The audience booed as they dragged him out. I watched with both admiration and pride.

It turned out that he was being chased for sneaking into the show, using the same method that he had used at Canucks games. He would wait for a family with at least three kids to approach the turnstile. Usually, the father of the family would be at the end of the line with the tickets, and his kids would be ahead of him. Mikey would walk to front of the family, pretending he was with them, and say, "My dad has the tickets," motioning to the back of the line. Once he was through, he would quickly blend into the crowd. By the time the confused dad explained that he had brought only three kids, not four, Mikey would be long gone. This method had worked before, but there was always the risk that it could end in a chase. Lucky for us, when he tried it at the John Byner show, it resulted in a legendary pursuit.

My cousin Ed, Mikey's younger brother, was also no stranger to being chased around the Coliseum. The difference was that he would sneak into an empty building during the day to watch some of his favourite hockey teams practising. As Montreal Canadiens fan, he started skipping school in Grade 7 to go down to the Coliseum on game day to see their morning practices whenever they were in town. These practices were not open to the public but, as Ed tells me, "There is always a way in." They would check for unlocked doors, which were rare, as most were chained shut from the inside on game days. If they couldn't find an open one, they would pull on the handles and squeeze their smallest friend, "Munch," between the cracks of the chained doors. Munch, whose diminutive stature earned him the *Wizard of Oz*–themed nickname, would force himself through the tiny opening and find another door to pop open for the guys to rush in through.

These twelve- and thirteen-year-olds would sneak around the rink, avoiding the two security guards, who often chased them around the building. Ed and his friends would find a spot in the upper bowl (the "blues") and watch their heroes. When the practice was ending, the boys would head down to ice level to try to get autographs or sticks from the players. Most of the players were happy to see young fans, but some were less enthusiastic. Ed recalls one time, after being chased around, when he and his friends found a spot to hide under the bleachers. Bob Dailey, a Canuck at the time, pointed them out to the ushers, who grabbed the kids and put them in a golf cart to escort them out. When they approached the exit, the boys jumped out of the cart, and the pursuit started all over again. Another time, when the Pittsburgh Penguins were practising, Ed and his friends were waiting at ice level to meet the players. A skilled French Canadian member of the Penguins was showing off some of his fancy stickhandling when Ed made his friends laugh by calling out, "You think you're good? I can do that!" The player did not see the humour. He made eye contact with the twelve-year-old and yelled, "FUCK OFF!" Ed still seems a little surprised at the player's words, but also admits, "I was a cocky little bastard, and so was he, so it wasn't going to end well."

Years later, I found out that there were much less stressful ways to get into the Coliseum for free. One way was to know the doorman who worked at the entrance of Center Ice, the "premium" restaurant at the Coliseum. If you gave him the heads-up that you wanted to get into a game, he could let you in, provided you weren't wearing jeans. So, I would call my friend Chris, who worked at the door, and head down to the rink in the only pair of dress pants I owned.

When I was in university, my friend Ross got me a job working at the Coliseum, delivering food to the private suites during Canucks games and concerts. I would finish my deliveries by the end of the first period, so I could stay and watch two thirds of the game for free—if I wanted to. It might be hard to believe now, but most days I just went home after the first period to beat the rush. When I started working at the Coliseum in 1988, the Canucks were not a hot ticket in town. Vancouver didn't have any real pride or confidence in the Canucks until the Trevor Linden– and Pavel Bure–led teams in the 1990s. It's true that they made it to the finals in 1982, and the city enjoyed the

Gino Odjick of the Canucks (second from left) with the doormen
of the Center Ice Restaurant at the Coliseum.
COURTESY OF CHRIS GIELTY.

ride, but the Canucks were outclassed by the much superior New
York Islanders team before returning to their losing ways. Many long-
suffering Canucks fans will swear that there has been a loyal fan base
for years, and to a degree, they're right. But I also know that when I
started working at the Coliseum, it was easier to find an empty seat at
a Canucks game than on the bus ride home.

On a few of the occasions when I stayed to watch a game, I had
postgame drinks and snacks in the owner's suite with some of the
other restaurant employees. Were we invited to do so by the owners,
the Griffiths family, for doing such a good job? Not really. It was
more like sneaking alcohol from your parents and replacing it with
water, except we didn't replace it with anything. We would sit in the
suite high above the ice surface, eating any untouched food that I had
delivered earlier and drinking beer out of the team owner's mini-bar.

I spoke to Brian, a cousin of my friend Chris, about his time working at the Coliseum in the mid-1970s, about a decade before I worked there. In my job I had limited interaction with the public, as I was delivering food to private suites, but Brian was always in contact with the customers; he was one of the "Dueck boys," the vendors who walked through the sections selling pop and snacks. They wore shirts that said "Dueck" on the back—one of the sponsors was the local Dueck car dealership. Brian started working just months after emigrating from Scotland when he was fourteen, and he stayed in the job until he was seventeen. Although Brian spent most of his time vending at the Coliseum, he also sold snacks at the Agrodome, Empire Stadium, and the Gardens, where during wrestling matches, he often witnessed an old lady in the front row beating the wrestlers with her umbrella whenever they fell outside of the ring. In the Coliseum, the Dueck boys were only allowed to sell snacks to people in the cheap seats in the blues. The lower seats, the reds, were filled with season ticket holders, who presumably didn't want their view blocked by a teenager slinging sodas. The working-class guys who sat in the back rows of the upper blues were the ones who treated Brian the best. They would bring mickeys of rum and whisky with them, and Brian would sell them half-full pops so they could fill the rest with booze. They were also the only guys who ever tipped.

Brian always worked with his cousin, Tommy, who had also emigrated from Scotland. Brian describes their relationship as being "like brothers" and says Tommy was possibly the toughest guy he'd ever known. And when these two hardworking Scottish "brothers" carried trays of snacks around games and concerts at the Coliseum, there were times when Tommy "acted gallus," a Scottish way of saying he was bold and unafraid. Brian claims that Tommy never went looking for a fight but was always ready if one came to him. One of the times it came to him was in the form of Peter Frampton. In 1975, on the tour before Frampton became one of the biggest rock stars in the world, he was playing a show at the Coliseum, opening for Montrose and Black Oak Arkansas. While Frampton was doing his sound check, he made fun of Brian and Tommy as they passed with their trays of snacks. Brian explains how things quickly got heated:

> And as we're about twenty yards away, [Peter Frampton] goes, "Check. Check one, two." And he sees us. Then he goes, "Popcorn! Peanuts! Ice cream!"
>
> By now we're about five yards away. And my cousin and I just let go. We're like, "Fuck you, you English fucker. Come on down here and say that to us. Come on, you fucker! Let's go!" And over the microphone, he shouts, "Oh my god, they're Scottish!" He's never thinking in a million years that he's gonna be in Vancouver with two sixteen- or seventeen-year-old Scottish guys calling him down.

I asked what Tommy would have done if Frampton had come down, and Brian said, "He would have killed him!"

Tommy's gallus behaviour was not reserved for effete English rock stars, however. Sometimes audience members also had to be set straight. The boys sold cups of pop and had to carry thirty at a time. Twenty would fit in the tray, and ten more could be squeezed between them. Because they received commission as well as an hourly salary, they worked hard to sell as many drinks as possible. If they ever spilled a drink, they had to return the empty cup, otherwise they would have to pay for it. At a Pink Floyd show, also in 1975, a stoner tried to rip off Brian by not paying for two Cokes. When Brian pressed him for the money, the guy told him to fuck off. As Brian angrily walked away, Tommy happened to be coming toward him. Here is how Brian remembers it:

[Tommy] says, "What the hell? What's wrong? What's the problem?" And I told him, and he says, "Oh okay, all right. Okay," he says, and he's loaded up. He's got thirty pops around his neck, right? And he says, "Let's just walk up there ... Just point the guy out to me." So, we walk up, and the guy is about five rows up, six seats in. And I point the guy out. And my cousin just goes up, takes his tray, and just dumps them all over the guy, thirty pops. This was from head to toe, and all over his friends. And my cousin is only like sixteen at the time. This guy is at least twenty years old. And [Tommy] says, "If you get out of this chair, I'm going to kill you." And I'm like, oh my god, I'm gonna get killed myself here. But the guy can see it in my cousin's eyes. He wasn't stupid. Anyway, so we're standing there and the whole place is like, it's just like, everybody's quiet. Something's gonna happen. And next thing, my cousin says to him, "Start passing back the empty cups!" When he took the empty cups back, it meant we never had to pay for them ... Meanwhile, this guy is covered, and his friends are covered, completely in Coca-Cola and 7 Up from head to toe ... Can you imagine how sticky that would be?

Brian and Tommy stood there while the humiliated stoner and his friends passed back all thirty cups.

If you wanted something stronger than a pop at the Coliseum in the 1970s, you couldn't get it from the Dueck boys, as beer sales were very limited. For years, there were designated beer gardens in the Coliseum, the only places where you could consume alcohol. They had TV monitors to watch the game, but you were not allowed to take a drink to your seat unless you were in one of the corporate suites. The logic, I suppose, was that it was a family friendly event, and non-corporate Canucks fans couldn't be trusted to behave if they were allowed to drink in their seats. It was okay for a kid to watch two men on skates beat the shit out of each other as long as they weren't sitting near someone drinking overpriced beer. I once saw a fan try to take two drinks from the beer garden on the lower concourse to his seat. He walked past an usher, who told him to stop, and continued up the stairs. Immediately, a police officer leapt into action, grabbed the collar of the guy's leather jacket, and yanked him backward. The beer splashed out of the cups in foamy arcs as he was violently dragged down the stairs and thrown onto the concrete floor. He yelled and resisted as the cop twisted his hands behind his back and handcuffed him. I don't think he knew it was a policeman until he was in cuffs and rushed out of the building.

Not every ejection from the Coliseum was an overreaction, though. Sometimes it was well deserved. Take, for example, the guy who pulled Vince Neil, the lead singer of Mötley Crüe, off the stage. On November 12, 1985, Mötley Crüe was playing to a sold-out crowd at the Coliseum. Neil was singing the first verse of "Looks That Kill" at the front of the stage when he was grabbed by the ankle and thrown into the pit by one of his fans, bringing the concert to a halt. This anecdote was even covered in the bestselling Mötley Crüe book, *The Dirt*. What wasn't covered, however, was *why* he was dragged into the crowd. The answer is simple, if not obvious. It's because Neil was a pencil-neck.

It turns out that the fan who grabbed Neil and hurled him into the crowd was my friend Eric, from the roller coaster. He was standing in the front row, excited to see one of his favourite bands. When Neil planted a foot near the edge of the stage to take a rock star pose, Eric noticed how skinny he was and grabbed his leg. He told me, "I could fit my hand all the way around his ankle. It was pathetic. He was such a pencil-neck, I had to throw him." Eric was pounced on, dragged, punched, and kicked by a group of security guards before being tossed out one of the back doors. It was a concert he will never forget, even though he saw less than half of the first song.

Erika, a friend of mine, told me a concert story from the Coliseum that is the opposite of the Mötley Crüe tale. It was June 30, 1980, and Erika and her friend Leslie, both sixteen, were at the Coliseum to see Queen. They cheered with the sold-out crowd as the band played their big hits, including "We Will Rock You," "Killer Queen," and "Bohemian Rhapsody." The show ended with someone jumping up onstage to sing "We Are the Champions" with lead singer Freddie Mercury, who called off the security guards and put his arm around the fan. Carrying their ten-dollar souvenir programs, the girls made their way to the roadway behind the Coliseum, where they waited for Leslie's dad, who worked at the racetrack next to the arena. Just then, several cars carrying VIPs and members of the band came out from under the building. The last car, a black limousine, stopped beside the girls, and the rear window rolled down. Mercury leaned out and said, "Hi girls!"

"Hi," they replied, both stunned and confused about what was happening.

"Did you enjoy the show?" he asked.

"Yes, it was great," they managed to reply. They didn't think to ask for an autograph, and neither had a camera for a picture.

"Well, thanks for coming to the show!" Mercury said with a smile. The girls nodded and stared. "Have a good night," he said, as the limo started to pull away.

"Thanks!" they called after him, wondering if anyone would believe them.

So, in roughly the same spot, an overeager teenage fan got his ass kicked by security at one show, and two girls had a pleasant exchange with a rock star at another. Clearly, a kind interaction with a hero is preferable to a beating, but they're both good memories.

So, what is the best way to get into the Coliseum? Well, buying a ticket is probably the safest way, but looking a doorman right in the eye while walking in for free is better. And that's exactly what my cousin Ed did for years. After sneaking into all those hockey practices, Ed was ready for the big time. He was going to sneak into games. He was never interested in running when he could walk, so he found a way in that played to his strength: talking. Or, more specifically, bullshitting. Ed has always been willing to talk himself into or out of any situation. In this case, he simply had to convince a doorman that he played for the local junior hockey team, the New Westminster Bruins. One of the perks of playing on the team was free admission to Canucks games. It was convenient for Ed that his brother, Mikey, did actually play for the Bruins. It took just one trip to the Coliseum with his older brother to set the wheels in motion.

Mikey was going to a game one night in 1975 with another member of the Bruins when fourteen-year-old Ed decided to tag along. He put on Mikey's Bellingham Blazers hockey jacket, and they convinced the doorman that Ed had just made the team. As the Blazers were the farm team for the Bruins, the logic tracked. The doorman mentioned that Ed's name was not on the list, but his supposed recent call-up explained that omission. And that was the start of years of free games.

Ed knew that the way to keep getting in was to act like he was supposed to be there. He became friendly with the doorman, an older guy in his seventies, often patting him on the back and asking how he was. "Have a good night, boys!" the doorman would say to Ed and the friends he began to bring along. At one point, Ed was bringing up to seven other "players" to watch the game. They went to twenty or so games a year, for four years. They would have kept doing it, but some local ticket scalpers whom Ed had helped get into a few games tried the scam on their own and blew it for everyone. From that point on, a younger doorman took over and adhered strictly to the list, with no exceptions. "I knew it was over," Ed told me, "So I had to find another way in." He soon found it lying unattended on a desk in an open office at the Coliseum. It was a vendor pass. He slipped it into his pocket, and it let him in everywhere.

Ed showed me the pass, which he still has, when I was over at his house in the summer of 1978. He had used a razor blade to cut it open, replaced the picture with his own, and added a makeshift PNE pinwheel logo to make it look official. And, because it was a vendor pass of the type used by the Dueck boys, he could use it to get into the fair, Empire Stadium, the Coliseum, and just about anything that took place on the PNE property. It was a long way from sneaking his smallest friend through a chained door to see a practice, but the logic remained the same: there must be a way into this place. Just like I longed to find a way into the glamorous world of teenagers and Vancouver wanted a way into the club of world-class cities, Ed knew there was always a way into the Coliseum. And for all of us, it involved a lot of bullshit.

The pass my cousin Ed used to get into games and concerts for a year.
COURTESY OF ED PEROVICH.

CHAPTER 5

East Side Story

"The PNE was my playground from the time I was six until I was fourteen.
I honestly consider myself lucky to have grown up there."
—Dan

AT EIGHT YEARS OLD, Dan was watching a soccer game with his dad at Callister Park stadium, which was run by the PNE on a site directly across the street from the Pacific Coliseum. In 1968, the Pacific Coast League was the best soccer you could watch in Vancouver, played on a field that was primarily dirt and sand. The grass had long been worn away by rodeos and demolition derbies. This game was a fierce rivalry between Croatia and Columbus, the Italian team. All the players were local, but nationalism ran deep in the crowd and on the field. Dan's dad was the treasurer for Croatia, and one of his duties was to hold the players' wallets and watches in a bag during the game. When Croatia scored the first goal, their supporters went crazy, and the players rushed over to congratulate the goal scorer. The celebration was cut short when an angry Italian fan jumped onto the field and punched the Croatian player in the face. They began fighting, which quickly led to players pushing and shoving and fans from both sides rushing the field to join the brawl. Here is how Dan remembers it:

> There's a hundred people on the field, and next thing you know, my dad says to me, "Hold the bag!" He's gone. He hops over the fence. He's out there, fighting. I'm a little kid holding a bag full of watches and wallets, thinking, Oh geez, while I'm watching my old man scrap. They were really intense games.

Callister Park stadium, which had a five-thousand-seat capacity, was demolished in 1971, but anyone who ever went there still beams when they talk about it. It was an integral part of the community and brought fans, particularly East Side fans, together to share emotional and contentious times.

For many people in the city, the PNE is something that takes place over the last seventeen days of summer. When Dan was a kid in the 1960s and early '70s, most Vancouverites visited the fair once a year and occasionally came back for concerts or sporting events. The locals, however, especially the kids, saw the PNE grounds as an extension of their own backyards. "Nothing was locked," Dan tells me. As a kid, he would wander into Empire Stadium to collect soccer balls after a Whitecaps practice, go into the stables to look at the Clydesdales and chat up the 4-H girls, or slip into the Coliseum to watch a hockey practice. The PNE grounds were not a locked fortress with a prohibitive admission fee. If anything, they were the opposite. Not only did local kids feel comfortable on the grounds, but there was also a sense that they shouldn't have to pay for anything. And most of them never did.

The PNE was and still is the largest single employer of young people in the province. Over a thousand temporary staff, mostly teenagers, are needed each year to keep the fair running. In the 1980s, when I worked there, most of the kids were from the surrounding

A soccer game at Callister Park before all the grass was
worn away by rodeos and demolition derbies.
CITY OF VANCOUVER ARCHIVES 180-4020A.

neighborhood and were happy to give freebies to each other. Frank,
a local kid who started working at the PNE at age fourteen, explains
how local kids treated each other:

> My buddies would be working parking, so we'd be able
> to park for free. And then one of my best buddies worked
> the arcade, so he would open up the machines and *click,
> click, click,* and put ten credits up on the pinball machine
> or the foosball machine or the air hockey machine. And
> so, we played for free for hours, right? Then we'd go to
> whatever game another buddy was working on. You'd
> give the guy five bucks, and he gave back twenty. You
> would walk away with a prize and fifteen bucks in your

pocket. And then of course, you'd go to the concession, and there'd be somebody else from school working in the ice cream place, and you get a free ice cream. And it was all reciprocal. And then when he came to where I worked, I'd do the same thing. Do whatever we could for each other. Like I said, you'd park for free, eat for free, and play games for free. You got on rides for free. It was crazy.

Red, the arcade bouncer, remembers it the same way, "I used to give out a lot of free games and got some burgers and stuff in return. So, we all used to, you know, help each other out. In certain ways, when we worked, it was like a family, right?"

Frank also points out the role the PNE played in bringing together East Side kids from different schools, including some from neighbouring Burnaby:

We really started to connect with people from other schools. You know, you've got a few different schools that we got to hang out with, like the North Burnaby crowd. It brought Vancouver and Burnaby together. We were working with Tech guys, Notre Dame guys, Burnaby North and Burnaby South guys ...

Although I grew up in Vancouver's East Side, my neighbourhood in the Killarney area didn't feel like East Van to me at the time, even though it technically was. It wasn't until I was an adult that I expanded my definition of East Vancouver to include the southeast part of the city. The traditional view of East Van is more the northeast section of the city. However, the major divide in Vancouver has always been an east/west one, and anyone who has lived east of Main Street is aware which side they are on. When I worked at the PNE with kids from all the different East Side schools, I felt the same connection that Frank talks about.

Both Dan and Frank stressed how the PNE was economically important to families in the area. Kids were able to make a few extra dollars to help with clothes at the beginning of the school year, which took some of the strain off their parents. Dan explains:

> For a lot of the kids in the neighborhood, we were from families that really didn't have a lot of disposable income. So, the beginning of the school year was a burden on parents. Because, you know, your kids want to have new jeans. They want to have runners. You want to go to your first day of school wearing your new clothes, right? And so, I was able to buy myself some Adidas runners and Levi's jeans.

This is a common story among people I talked to who lived in the area and worked at the fair as teens. Their fathers, often recent immigrants, worked in labour jobs that only provided enough to make ends meet. Frank says, "It created economic opportunities for east end kids at a time when there weren't a lot." These temporary jobs also provided teens with the opportunity to fool around, scam, and avoid actually working.

Dan was hired as a sweeper when he was fourteen and still looks back on the job fondly. It wasn't because he loved custodial work; he just liked having the opportunity to wander around different buildings and talk to girls. His boss was referred to at the time as "a little slow," and the teenage sweepers took advantage of his short memory. Some of the guys would punch in, work for a bit, then leave for a few hours. They might go home and sleep or meet up with friends— mainly things that didn't involve cleaning up other people's garbage. When they came back, they would pretend they had been there the whole time. If the boss asked why he hadn't seen them for hours, they would reply, "What are you talking about? I just talked to you an hour ago." This was usually enough to get them off the hook, though

Dan remembers a lot of guys getting fired for being terrible employees. "Half of these sweepers would routinely just get fired all the time because guys were fucking around so much. But somehow, I managed to avoid it. And I think I worked there for three or four years. And it was a great job. I think I was getting paid like three bucks an hour or something like that. But still, that was actually pretty good money."

Not only did the fair offer the local kids some pocket money and a place to bond, the PNE grounds provided them with a year-round playground. Among the organized activities, there was weekly roller skating at Rollerland in the 1970s, which Dan never missed.

> We would go there every Wednesday night, and I couldn't roller skate worth a shit, but I still went because you got to meet girls there. And I remember they would always have a "couples only" skate. It was the first time I ever held a girl's hand. You had to ask a girl if she wanted to skate with you, and then you held her hand. You did a few laps, and when the song was over, went back to open skating again. You'd be so excited about going to Rollerland because you would get to meet some girls.

Not every interaction on the PNE grounds was as pleasant for Dan as the first time he held a girl's hand, though. He spent a lot of time in the Coliseum watching Canucks practices and would often get autographs, pucks, and even sticks from players. But when he was twelve, he helped himself to a broken goalie stick that he saw outside the Canucks locker room. He assumed that the goalie wouldn't want the stick since the blade was cracked in half. Dan was walking away with it when he was suddenly confronted.

> He comes out of the dressing room and goes, "HEY, YOU LITTLE FUCKER! GIVE ME MY STICK BACK!"
> And I'm thinking, Okay, I can outrun this guy. So, I bolt.

I started running across the PNE. By the time I got to Empire Stadium, he was like five feet behind. I thought, He's gonna catch me. He's right behind me, yelling and swearing at me. Finally, I just think, I gotta drop this stick. I gotta get away from this guy. And so ultimately, I just dropped the stick. He picked it up and stopped chasing me. To this day I think, What a prick! Here I am, a little kid just trying to have a broken goalie stick.

To give some perspective, if you are not familiar with the layout of the PNE grounds, the Coliseum and Empire Stadium were as far apart as you could get. The chase was equivalent to about eight city blocks. I'm sure there were weekly, if not daily instances of kids getting chased off the property by angry adults. Dan says, "There was no security there. It wasn't fenced. The grounds were wide open. You could pretty much walk into any venue at any time. Even at the Coliseum, if you checked every door, which we did, there was always one that was unlocked."

Somehow, Dan managed to have an even scarier encounter with another professional athlete. He was a fan of All Star Wrestling, which took place at the PNE Gardens. He would watch it on TV on Saturday mornings, even though it was happening just blocks from his house. One of the wrestlers was named the Belgian Beast, and Dan says the rumour at the time was that the Beast had killed a man in the ring. This never actually happened, but once a rumour starts with kids, it's impossible to stop. Then, one day, the Beast moved two houses away from Dan. It was exciting to have a professional wrestler as a neighbour, but Dan often got into conflicts with the Belgian Beast's son.

He had a kid that was the same age as me, and [we] always used to fight. It always used to start because this kid would give me like a fucking arm bar, like a wrestling hold or something. And it would hurt. He would hurt me. And then I would manage to get out of the hold, and then I'd kick his ass. And then he would run home and cry. One time, and this is a vivid memory for me, I was in my neighbour's yard, the house in between ours and the Belgian Beast's house, [with these kids] Jimmy and Johnny. And we were playing. Then the Beast comes after me. Don't get me wrong. I didn't hurt [his] kid. It was just, you know, [he got] punched in the nose. [The Beast] came out after me. And I'll never forget: he was chasing me, and I was climbing over the fence to go into my yard. And he was close to grabbing me. I was quick enough that he couldn't get me. But fuck, I pissed my pants climbing over the fence. He never did come into my yard because I guess he realized he couldn't beat a ten-year-old kid. Yeah, but oh my God, was I scared. I thought, This guy who's famous for killing a man in the ring is now chasing me because I punched out his son.

The local kids never really shied away from the dangers of wandering the PNE grounds because the potential payoffs were worth it. Dan was so comfortable at the park that he walked right onto the track at Empire Stadium to try to get Pelé's autograph before a soccer game. Even though Pelé was considered the greatest soccer player of all time, no security stopped Dan from approaching him. Another time, after watching a Canucks practice, the kids inside the Coliseum were told that they had to leave because the Boston Bruins practice, which was supposed to start right after, had been cancelled. To encourage everyone to leave, the lights were turned out in the building after the Canucks left the ice. Dan and his friend didn't believe that the practice was really cancelled, so they decided to lie down on the ground in the upper-level seats and wait. They lay there in complete darkness for over half an hour before the lights came back on and some of the

Dan (right) with his cousin in Empire Stadium.
COURTESY OF DAN STEFAN.

Bruins, including Bobby Orr, hit the ice. Dan and his friend sat up and commented that they must be the only people in there. Within a few seconds, however, they saw about a hundred other kids popping up around the rink. They had all been waiting in the complete blackout. The young fans were rewarded for their patience and got to watch the practice—some even got souvenir sticks from the Bruins. Dan is still in awe of the fact that he got to meet so many of his heroes on the PNE grounds.

Frank also found a way to get close to some of his idols at the PNE. He and a friend scammed their way into a Queen concert at the Coliseum by hanging around the will call booth, reading a ticketholder's name on an envelope, and claiming the tickets as their own. They were surprised to see that the tickets came with what they thought at first were souvenir stickers but were actually backstage passes. The teenage boys nervously approached the backstage area and flashed the passes at a guard, who said to stick them to their thighs as he waved them through. A member of the crew mistook them for actual workers and called out, "Hey, you two! Move these cases over there!" Frank and his friend did what they were told and found themselves in a small hallway at the side of the stage. Then, Freddie Mercury appeared just a few feet away from them. As the members of Queen walked out to an ovation, the boys moved to the side of the stage to watch the first two songs before returning to the audience to avoid getting caught.

There was a sense of entitlement many East Van kids had which contributed to the level of risk they were willing to take on the PNE grounds. It created a culture where they felt completely comfortable, almost justified in their actions. People who were happy to help themselves to free games, prizes, and money at the PNE wouldn't have done the same at other jobs. Some of the scams were inventive and brazen, like the one I was told about that went on in the beer garden. Although the kegs of beer in the tent were provided by the PNE, some guys would bring in extra kegs to sell. The money from those kegs was not recorded, and at the end of each day a few employees would split the cash profits. Technically, I guess they weren't really stealing anything as they were selling their own beer, but I'm sure it wasn't legal—the same way I can't set up a table and sell my own wine at the liquor store. To the guys, however, it was just a part of the unspoken understanding many East Van residents had about their time on the PNE grounds.

East Vancouver, especially the area surrounding the PNE, traditionally has a reputation as being the rougher part of the city. This dates to a time when cheaper housing was on the outskirts of the developing town. It was an industrial area too, including the city docks where my dad and uncles worked as longshoremen. Some areas of East Vancouver were genuinely dangerous, and that reputation stuck for many years. Many long-term East Vancouver residents have embraced that identity, but it has also been adopted by more affluent residents who have moved into the area in the last decade or so. You see them on Commercial Drive, wearing T-shirts based on the huge piece of public art that bears the unofficial East Vancouver logo—a simple cross with "EAST" written vertically and "VAN" written horizontally. As a teenager, I used to see the East Van cross spray-painted on schools, written on desks, and carved into washroom stalls long before it became official public art. I remember hearing a story about a guy who got it tattooed on his arm but was forced to have it removed after some East Side tough guys decided he wasn't worthy. I know the meaning of the East Van cross has changed over the years, but so has East Vancouver. It has evolved and now includes an active arts community that my wife and I have enjoyed for years. From comedy shows and poetry slams on Commercial Drive to plays at the Cultch and concerts at the Waldorf and the Rio, East Van has become a vibrant part of the city's identity.

The historical reputation of East Vancouver as a tough place goes both ways, though. There have always been people who look down at the residents of East Vancouver as crass, unrefined, and basic. Frank recalls how difficult it used to be for East Van kids to find a place for themselves in the west side of the city.

> There weren't a lot of opportunities for us. You know, people don't remember what it was like. We got the tail end of it. Guys who are about ten or fifteen years older than us had a tough time. You know, there was a stigma around East Vancouver, and they had a tough time just heading west of Main.

When I spoke to former Vancouver Whitecap Bob Lenarduzzi, he echoed the same sentiment.

> When I got older and was starting to venture outside of East Vancouver, it was actually quite humorous when somebody asked you where you grew up and [after I told them, they'd say,] "Oh my God, that's dangerous there." I remember thinking, No, it's not, actually. But it had a reputation … I think the reputation was unwarranted. But it was just amazing to me how often it would come up. [They'd ask,] "Did you ever get in any fights?"

When Dan was nine years old, he watched a thoroughbred race-horse running down his street, five blocks from the Hastings racetrack on the PNE grounds. This horse, among dozens of others, was running wild in the city after being freed from a burning barn at the track. A barricade was set up on the Second Narrows Bridge to stop the horses from running to North Vancouver. Police corralled three horses racing down Hastings Street. For the residents of the area, it was just another day living next to the PNE. Whether it was a racehorse galloping down your street, a professional wrestler chasing you through a yard, or the sound of a cheering crowd from the nearby stadium, for locals like Dan and Frank, it was impossible to escape the fact that their neighbourhood just wasn't like anywhere else in the city.

CHAPTER 6

Diane

WHEN I WAS A KID in the 1970s, our annual family trip to the fair at the PNE was one of the best parts of my summer. We'd pile into my mom's 1969 Dodge Coronet 500, and my brother, sister, and I would enjoy the fifteen-minute drive unencumbered by seat belts, which we only used once a year when we drove to Birch Bay, Washington. I was never into the scary rides at the PNE (just the seat belt-less drive for me, thanks!), but always looked forward to the games, junk food, and entertainment. My sister and I loved to spin around on the Tilt-A-Whirl and slide on burlap sacks down the impossibly tall Giant Slide. We marvelled at the lumberjack show as competitors scurried up thirty-metre (hundred foot) poles, ran on spinning logs in the water in attempt to topple their opponents, and carved tiny chairs out of stumps with chainsaws. We all laughed and cheered as the demolition derby drivers rammed into each other until only one sputtering car spewing black smoke limped around in a victory lap. And we craved the food: minidonuts, buttery scones filled with jam, and greasy hamburgers.

I liked all these things almost as much as I hated the PNE Prize Home. Our parents would force us to wait in line for what seemed like hours to be herded through a house that was being raffled off. It

My mom outside her house on Pender Street in the early 1940s.
COURTESY OF NICK MARINO.

wasn't a special house, at least not to me, but my parents seemed to be excited about a dishwasher or a bay window. It was classic adult bullshit at the time, like green peppers on a pizza. It seemed like they were being purposely contrarian by keeping me hostage in a boring house when the world outside was buzzing, flashing, and ringing. I just wanted to get to some of those carnival games that the adults kept telling me were a waste of money.

The possibility of winning something, especially a stuffed animal, was the best part of the day. Every year I would add a couple more to my collection. We'd get five dollars each to play as many games as we could, which was ten or so at the time, and trade up for better and better prizes. When I was seven, I won two 750 mL (25 oz) glass bottles of Pepsi at a ring toss game, along with a plush toy. Miraculously, my mom let me keep the Pepsi—she tended to ration our junk food. I still remember how great that warm pop tasted as I drank a glass of it in my bedroom, looking out at the summer night slowly fading through my window. Sitting on my bed, I asked my mom if the group of trees I could see in the distance was Vancouver Island. It was just Central Park, a forty-minute walk from our house, but sometimes when you're young the world can seem so small and so big at the same time. I fell asleep with the new stuffed animal under my arm, a dog in overalls with the name "Clem" written on his chest. Sure, it started to leak stuffing within a few weeks, but that night I held on to it like a piece of a day that I didn't want to let go.

Occasionally, my parents ended up at the PNE on their own, though this was rare, as we tended to do most things as a family. One time, they went to see a show that was part of the PNE's Star Spectacular concert series and decided to walk around the fairgrounds for a bit. They stopped at the over/under dice game to make a few bets. My dad's childhood best friend, Tony, was working the game. As they placed bet after bet, Tony made sure that they were paid out, regardless of which numbers were rolled. Their luck continued at another

Lumberjacks in the Timber Show pole-climbing competition.
CITY OF VANCOUVER ARCHIVES 180-7392.

game when my dad won a jumbo stuffed St. Bernard by tossing a dime onto a lipless plate. Somehow, it did not slide off like the thousands of dimes before it. As it was one of those seemingly impossible games, no trading up was necessary. He was immediately awarded the giant prize.

I love thinking about my mom and dad walking through the fair, holding a jumbo stuffed dog. To be honest, I don't have a lot of images of my parents on their own in my head. The fact that they had a life outside of the family, before or during the lives of their kids, was always weird to me. When they brought the stuffed St. Bernard home, it was hard to believe it was real. They had somehow found a way to do what every kid who walks through that gate dreams of. It was proof that anything is possible, that dreams really can come true. I know I'm overreacting, but it was *that* exciting. The novelty of having a gigantic plush toy in the house wore off pretty quickly, but it did remain a symbol of the magic out there. If my dad could win one of these, who knew what else was possible? At the time to me, it was the most impressive thing my dad had ever done.

A few years ago, someone said to my sister, "I remember your family. You always sat on your front steps together, eating cherries and spitting the pits into the yard." I can remember doing that a few times, for sure, though it doesn't feel like a defining quality of my family. But I've learned that you can't choose how you are remembered. My aunt once told me about a relative of ours who had to be carried out of a bar directly to the hospital because his hemorrhoids were so bad. He may have done some great things in his life, but all I really know is that his ass once hurt so bad his friends had to lug him from a bar stool to an operating table. I could have asked my aunt a few follow-up questions, but I felt like she'd already given me all the relevant details. He didn't get to choose how he was remembered, and I guess my family doesn't either. If that means we are thought of as the family who spent summer nights on our front steps sharing a bowl of cherries, I'll take it. A family goes through plenty of phases and shifting dynamics, as I would soon find out. I like the idea of one of our phases being as peaceful as that scene on the steps.

My mom was diagnosed with cancer in the summer of 1976, just before I turned nine and shortly after a family road trip to Disneyland. My mom loved to drive—she'd been doing it since she was fourteen. She drove every mile of the trip to California and back, while my dad often slept in the passenger seat. When we returned, she had

In a photo booth with my sister, Angela (left), and brother, Mike (right).
COURTESY OF MIKE MARINO.

a gigantic mole removed from her shin. Testing confirmed that she had melanoma. We never called it cancer. It was just "mom's sickness." She was a private person and wouldn't have liked the attention that a public broadcasting of that diagnosis would have brought. Life went on. She drove us to soccer and lacrosse games, made our meals, played cards with us, and made popcorn when we watched *The Carol Burnett Show*. We never thought she would die, though there were brief moments when I allowed myself to consider the possibility. She had operations and began to walk with a limp. She asked about having her leg amputated to stop the spread, but the doctors didn't think it was a good idea. Still, I never heard her complain. It was her sickness, and she never put it on anyone else. Like a lot of families who have a member battling cancer, we just continued doing what we had always done together. One of the main things we did as a family was go to watch the Vancouver Whitecaps soccer team at Empire Stadium, at the eastern edge of the PNE grounds.

We'd park blocks away from the stadium, and often my dad would point out the house he and his brother had bought for their mom in the 1950s with the money they made working on fishing boats and deep-sea vessels. Or sometimes we would drive by the block of Pender Street, where my mom and dad grew up as neighbours, just two blocks from the PNE. They'd known each other since they were in elementary school. In fact, my dad actually took my mom's sister to their Grade 9 graduation ceremony at Templeton Junior High. That was his last year of formal education before getting a job as a mess boy on a ship bound for England. It was the beginning of his life as a seaman, seeing the world. When he returned home in 1960, he saw my mom for the first time in a few years and asked her out. They were married two years later, and by 1967, when I was born, our family of five was complete. For a while, we all had season tickets for the Whitecaps, until my brother lost interest in the team. The four of us kept going, and the team continued getting better. The Whitecaps were great in 1978, though they didn't go far in the playoffs. The next year, however, would be very different.

In 1979, the Whitecaps won the Soccer Bowl, the championship game of the North American Soccer League. It was a huge deal in a city that had given up any hope of the Canucks or even the BC Lions winning a championship in the foreseeable future. The team that played their home games deep in the east side of the city were welcomed as hometown heroes at the airport when they arrived from New York after defeating the Tampa Bay Rowdies 2–1. A downtown victory parade was attended by a hundred thousand fans, which is an amazing number considering the population of Vancouver at the time was only 425,000. It ended at Robson Square, in the heart of downtown, and I was there with my mom and my sister, Angela. There was even some preshow fun when a drunk fan climbed onto the edge of the glass dome above the stage. The audience started chanting "Jump! Jump! Jump!" which made Angela and me laugh. In response to the chant, the drunk put down the beer he was holding, balanced himself on the metal beam, stuck out his middle finger, and shouted, "FUCK YOU ALL!" to a chorus of laughter. I don't remember anything the Whitecaps team members said when they came up to the microphone later in the day, but I will never forget the image and the message of that foul-mouthed drunk. Somehow, it made a great day even better.

The Whitecaps Soccer Bowl victory was a highlight of my twelfth year and a pivotal moment in the history of Vancouver. In the game that the Whitecaps played to get into the final, they had faced the mighty New York Cosmos, the richest and most well-known team in the whole league. Somehow, through an improbable series of events, the Whitecaps tied the game, then won a second minigame, shocking the soccer world and securing a berth in the final. Jim McKay, a broadcaster for ABC Sports, was reflecting on the importance of the win for Vancouver when he said THE WORD.

Village.

He called Vancouver a *village*.

And for some reason, it made lots of people really angry—the sort of anger some adults still carry with them today when they hear the name Jim McKay. Obviously, no one really thought Vancouver was a village, but the implication that we were small-time, that we didn't sit at the big boys' table, really upset many Vancouverites. This was the moment when Vancouver decided that we wanted to be a world-class city, dammit! Or maybe we already were a world-class city! It wasn't clear. But we sure as hell weren't a village just because some dumb American said we were. No way! It was the start of a decades-long identity crisis for the city, the shadow of which still looms over us. Even now there are "It Takes a Village!" banners at Whitecaps home games—forty-four years after McKay's slight.

Vancouver wouldn't have to wait long for the opportunity to prove we belonged in the big leagues. In November 1980, Expo 86 was awarded to the city. At the time, it was called Transpo 86, based on its transportation theme, but it was soon upgraded to a World's Fair and renamed. Mike Harcourt, mayor-elect at the time of the announcement, had run on an anti–Transpo 86 platform, promising to cancel the event if he was elected. He promptly changed his mind after he won. Harcourt was suddenly on board for Transpo 86, due in part to the fact that the provincial government refused to fund rapid transit (the SkyTrain) unless he agreed to it. Also, the federal government wouldn't contribute to the construction of BC Place stadium unless he was on board with the six-month exposition. His hands were tied, but it must have been disappointing for people who had voted for him because of his anti-Transpo stance. (Harcourt would go on to become premier of the province, so his flip-flop on Transpo didn't really hurt him politically.)

Another future BC premier, Gordon Campbell, was quite outspoken about both Expo and Vancouver's status as a world-class city. Six months before Expo 86 opened, when he was a Vancouver city councillor, Campbell said, "I'm tired of telling others we're a world-class city. Let's go out and do it and let other people tell us we are world class." He seemed to take on this ambassador role as part of his life's work, making global headlines in Hawaii for drunk driving and London for an accusation of sexual misconduct. You can't say he didn't walk the walk, even if he couldn't walk a straight line. He went out there and showed everyone what his version of world class looks like. And, really, isn't it just about entitlement? The label of "world-class city" promises more opportunities for the citizens, but who really benefits? Is it the Vancouverites who now have the opportunity to live paycheque to paycheque in one of the least affordable cities in the world? Expo changed our city forever. Whether it made Vancouver world class, unaffordable, or both is up for debate.

As the city slowly changed around us, everything changed quickly for my family on February 7, 1981. I was downstairs in my room, sick with the flu, when I heard a loud bang on the ceiling, louder than any noise I had ever heard in the house before. I lay in bed, scared, confused, and dizzy. I tried to get up but could only sit on the edge of my bed while feet scurried above me. I heard sirens coming down our street and forced myself to get up. I said to myself, "If the sirens go past our house, Mom will live." It was a game I had been playing in my head for years. If this happens, then that will happen—there was no logic to it. I'm not sure why I made the stakes so high this time. I guess I knew that my mom was getting worse.

The sirens didn't go past our house that night. They stopped right in front. When I finally made it upstairs in a daze, there were firemen in my parents' bedroom and spilling out into the hall. A couple of them were standing in our hallway, having a casual conversation. I walked into her room, and she was lying on the floor, unconscious. The noise I had heard was my mom falling out of bed. I don't know if something had happened to make her fall or if she'd thrown herself out as a call for help. I was only in her room for a few seconds before I was led out. Soon she was put on a stretcher, taken out the front door, and lifted into an ambulance. My sister and I watched from the window as a neighbour hugged my dad on the boulevard in the glow of the ambulance lights.

Over the previous few weeks, my mom had rarely gotten out of bed. Some days she asked me to come home right after school to spend time with her. Sometimes I did, but not always. When I did, I would lie next to her in bed, and we'd talk about my day. I didn't realize that she was just trying to spend a bit more time with me before she died. I can still remember sitting on a bench outside of C gym at Killarney, talking to a girl on a day I had told my mom I would come home early. I couldn't pull myself away, however. For years, the thought of my mom waiting for me to come home as she lay in bed, slowly dying, has filled me with regret.

I didn't go to the hospital to see her on the first day, as I was still sick. My brother told me that they had to restrain my mom in her bed because she kept trying to get up and walk out. When I finally saw her a couple of days later, it was like seeing a different person. She was heavily medicated, forgetful, and tired. At home, she was the one in charge, but here she seemed confused and weak. My siblings and I had stilted conversations with her as she drifted in and out of sleep. It was her, but she wasn't really there, and she never would be again. I remember whispering, "I love you, mom," to her as she was sleeping, possibly the only time I ever said it to her. I may have written it on a Mother's Day card I made in school, but it just wasn't something we said. She used to play the Paul Simon song "Loves Me Like a Rock," which details a mother's unwavering love for her child, and tell me that was how she felt about me. That was as close as we ever got to verbalizing our feelings.

Seeing her so weak was strange because she had always been the strong one, the one in control. She wasn't like a typical mom. I never saw her wear makeup or jewellery. She liked to watch football and boxing, loved Muhammad Ali. She had a great sense of humour, and I remember her getting us out of bed to watch Andy Kaufman on TV. But as much as she liked to laugh and to have fun, she also didn't take any shit. When I was five, I was in the car with her in the Killarney Community Centre parking lot. A group of slow-moving teenage girls sauntered in front of our car, laughing and smoking. My mom honked, and they looked back, smirked, and kept slowly walking, completely blocking our way. My mom drove closer to the group, just inches from the ringleader, who shot one more condescending look at my mom as she continued to casually strut in front of the car, proud of the inconvenience she was causing. This was too much for my mom. She tapped the gas and hit this girl right in the ass with her car, not hard enough to hurt her, but enough to change her attitude. The girl screamed and stumbled out of the way. The rest of the group parted in panic, and my mom drove off to a chorus of swearing and middle fingers. That's the version of Diane Marino I was used to, not the confused one in the hospital bed.

I returned to school a few days later, and it was surprisingly easy to get back into the swing of things. I liked the feeling of doing the same things I had always done. I was able to make jokes with my friends and pretend that everything was normal, but it really wasn't. My mom started getting treatments that made her quickly lose her hair. She became weaker and weaker, less aware of our presence. Even though it was clear she wasn't going to make it, we were still in denial. I remember Angela asking my dad if he and Mom would move into a smaller house when they got older, which was clearly never going to happen. My dad, struggling to be positive, said that he thought they might do that, and we pretended to believe him. Even now, over forty years later, my dad tells me that he didn't really think that she was going to die. At some point he must have realized that it might happen, because I was there with him and my aunt while they tried to get my mom to sign a will. She couldn't even hold a pen, so my aunt had to wrap her hand around my mom's to sign the document for her. I looked at it disapprovingly and thought, That doesn't look anything like her signature. Every time I visited her, there was less of her there. Soon she would just be a part of our memories.

I was sitting in English class in Mr. Kelsey's portable when there was a knock at the door, and I was asked to come out. My dad was waiting outside, and I walked over, knowing what was about to happen. "She passed away this morning," is all I remember him saying. I cried as we walked to the car and for the whole way home. Inside, I sat on the edge of my bed with my sister and took my shoes off really slowly as we both cried. We just sat there in tears, her hand on my back as I unlaced my high-top runners, looking at them as if there were some sort of importance in the act, as if anything mattered anymore.

We stayed home from school for a week, and then it was back to our usual routines, but nothing was the same. Everything took on some sort of elevated importance in the wake of her death. I broke a measuring cup while I was doing the dishes and cried, as if another connection to her was gone. I was careful, almost superstitious, when doing anything again for the first time since she died. When I went to play my first record, I saw AC/DC on the turntable and immediately took it off. It just felt disrespectful. In a stairwell at school, I ran into a girl I was going out with. She looked uncomfortable to see me and said she had heard about my mom. I thanked her and said I didn't think I wanted to go out anymore. She agreed, and we just moved on, just went to class. I could sense that people were looking at me differently, but no one really said anything. One guy, a kid named Dave who was a year older, came up to me, put his arm around my shoulder, and said sincerely, "I heard the news about your mom, and I wish it was otherwise." He was the only person I knew who directly addressed what had happened, and it meant a lot to me. Lots of people were extra nice at the time, but it is a difficult thing to bring up at that age. For the most part, I kept my feelings to myself at school, and when I was alone, I talked to my mom. I would talk out loud to her when I was walking home or when I was in my bedroom. I don't remember how it started, but it just became a thing I did.

One night, a couple of months after my mom died, I was hanging out with some kids from the Grade 9 basketball team and came home drunk. I had forgotten my key, and when my dad opened the door, he knew right away that I had been drinking. We argued a bit when I denied being drunk, and then I went downstairs to my room. I was talking out loud to my mom when my dad came in and asked who I was talking to. I said that I was talking to Mom and that I always did. He told me that she wouldn't have wanted me to do that and I should stop. I was angry, like he was trying to take her away, but I also felt like he was right. I closed my bedroom door, got into bed, and never spoke out loud to her again.

Although our family still existed, the version of it that we all knew died with my mom. My dad was suddenly the single parent of a thirteen-year-old, fifteen-year-old, and seventeen-year-old. He did a great job of trying to fill both parental roles. My mom had taught him to cook over the last couple of years, and he seemed to enjoy it. He made us feel protected and loved. Sometimes he would say, "It would have been easier if it was me who died. It's so much harder to lose your mom." I didn't like when he said that, but I understood what he meant and appreciated that he was saying he would have done anything for this to not to have happened to us. Within a few years, my brother moved out with his girlfriend, my sister moved in with my aunt, and my dad and I were the only two living in the house. Unlike the crowded PNE Prize Home that my parents dragged us through each year, our house was suddenly empty, and I was home alone a lot of the time in my teens. My unsupervised years began earlier than for most. I rarely brought report cards home, stayed out late on weekends, and began drinking with friends more often. I can't blame it all on the absence of my mom, however. My friends were doing a lot of the same things, and all their moms were alive.

My mom (right) and her sister, Dolores, in the late 1950s.
COURTESY OF MIKE MARINO.

CHAPTER 7

PNE Prize Home

FIVE MONTHS AFTER MY MOM DIED, when I was thirteen years old, I worked my second summer at the PNE. My dad's co-worker, Sam, moonlighted managing a bingo tent at the fair and offered me a job. It was a big switch from blowing up balloons all day, and I didn't have to dodge any darts. The downside, however, was that the clientele in the bingo tent was a lot different from people who tried to win records. Instead of watching teenagers laughing and cheering, I was now serving customers who were either elderly, down on their luck, or both. Rarely did teenage girls come to play bingo. Our tent was used as more of a respite than a destination. Overheated grandmas and their sweaty grandkids would flop down on stools to get out of the sun. Our customers seemed to have given up on the idea that they had any control over their experience at the PNE. It might as well be left to chance, like a goddamned bingo game. The kids at the other games still had hope and joy in them, but bingo players seemed like they were just marking time at a game where one person wins and everybody else loses. Players were either mad at the caller for not saying their numbers, at the winner for taking away their chance at a prize, or at themselves for coming to the fair. I collected their money, sat in my chair, and watched the fair pass me by while the players listlessly marked their cards with the dejected indifference of the nursing sow in the farm building.

On the fifth day on the job, I was offered a chance to make some extra money on a tent-wide scheme. I guess stealing had been such an issue at bingo in the past that a job existed solely to stop employees from pocketing money. It was one person's responsibility to write down exactly how many cards were sold for each game. At the end of the day, the tally on the sheet had to match the money in your apron. It seems like a good idea in theory, but it just made the crime more organized. Instead of people going rogue and taking random amounts each day, now there was planning and co-operation among

A bingo tent on the midway.
CITY OF VANCOUVER ARCHIVES 180-7380.

co-workers. Whoever was recording that day would quietly go to each collector and decide on how many cards they would leave off the total. That amount of cash would be tucked into waistbands or tube socks. Later, the stolen cash would be divided at a meeting spot in the park. Everyone wanted the recording job because they worked with four collectors, which could be quite lucrative if all of them were on board to skim and split a bit of money.

I was initiated by a blond girl a couple of years older than me. She casually leaned down and said, "Take forty dollars out. I'll leave it off this sheet. Meet me by the roller coaster after work. Twenty for you, twenty for me." She delivered all this while looking straight ahead, as if she were passing on the most trivial information and not pulling me back into the paranoia of stealing from work. I nodded and thought about a couple of records I might like to buy with the money. Then I put my hand in my apron and started folding a twenty-dollar bill into a little square with one hand while trying to look casual. When I mentioned this story to my sister, she said she had "learned to do origami" folding bills in her apron when she worked at the fair. I soon learned that every single worker in that bingo tent was in on it. Just a bunch of East Side kids making the most of an opportunity, I guess. There really wasn't any security at the fair in the early 1980s, so it wasn't that hard to get away with a scam. If you were subtle, the risk seemed low. There were unsubstantiated rumours, however, that if you did get caught, you would get the shit kicked out of you behind the roller coaster. Although I have since been assured that this wasn't true, I worried about it each time I slid another twenty-dollar bill into my pocket. In the end, the threat of being beaten and fired didn't seem to be enough of a deterrent for any of us to stop.

When my sister first started at the PNE, she was given advice on how to steal by a fellow employee, even though she wasn't planning to do it. She told me:

Because we worked for Gary, a co-worker told me to be
careful stealing money. I had never even thought to take
a dime. He told me that Gary marks the money. He said if
you ever need just one or two dollars, just take the ones.
Don't ever take a big bill.

I spoke to Isaac, a former games manager at the PNE, at his house
in East Vancouver. He started working at the fair in the 1950s and
stayed there well into the '80s, so our times overlapped. While I had
been dividing stolen money with co-workers by the roller coaster,
Isaac had been patrolling the midway, keeping an eye on the teenage
employees. I asked him what he did if he ever found people stealing
at the games, and he recounted a story about a young woman whom
he had to fire from a gambling tent.

She had clippers [tweezers]. You'd put money in the box,
but you couldn't take it out with your fingers. She went
and bought some long clippers. She used to put them in
and pull the money out, and I caught her. You see things
like this. I didn't hurt her. I just fire her and tell her it's
not the right way to do it. I say, "When you grow up, you're
gonna be a thief, you know." She was still a young lady. She
started crying. I said, "Don't cry. People got nature, you
know, it's in a person. You need the money, and you don't
know how to get it, so you try the best way you know how.
You found a way to do it, but it's not the right way."

Isaac was close friends with local gangsters ("they treated me like
family") and prides himself on his toughness and loyalty. He learned
that within organized crime, it is often better to settle a dispute without violence. In fact, the reason that Isaac had a job at the PNE at
all, according to him, was because he was able to solve a problem
between an acquaintance and the Mob.

Isaac with his ever-present cigar.
COURTESY OF ISAAC MESSINGER.

Isaac was ninety-three years old at the time of our interview and had a bit of trouble moving around, but he was eager to share his experiences with me. He was hard of hearing, struggled to recall certain dates and events, and stood barely over five feet tall. As I sat and listened to his stories, however, he seemed to become larger and larger. He was born in Poland in 1929 to Jewish parents, lost his whole family in the Second World War, and ended up living in several different orphanages. He got streetwise out of necessity, learned to fight, and formed a pickpocket partnership in which he provided the muscle if the pick went south. Soon he was accepted as an immigrant to Canada, lived with a Jewish family in Winnipeg, and made friends on the street. Some of these friends turned out to be connected to the Mafia, which started a lifelong association for Isaac. At one point in the early 1950s, an acquaintance named Jack came to Isaac, desperate for help. He was worried the Mob was going to kill him over an unpaid debt and wanted Isaac to intervene. Here is Isaac's version of the story:

> I got to know [Jack], and I could see the more I talk that the guy is not a bad guy. He's trying to save his life, you know. He had a family. He just about cry when he was talking. We met in a coffee shop, and I said, "Don't worry. I will try to straighten it out so the Mafia won't bother you, won't touch you." He didn't deserve to get hurt, so he didn't get hurt ... I got a good name about straightening things out ... So, when I come from Winnipeg, Jack already happen to be a boss at the PNE, so he give me the wheel, and he told me to keep all my money because I done him the favour years ago.

The "wheel" that Isaac is talking about is the crown and anchor gambling game at the fair. Not only did Jack help Isaac by giving him a job, he also told him to keep all the money that he took in each day, for the entirety of the fair. So, at the end of each shift, Isaac would pocket up to five hundred dollars—a huge amount of money at a time when the average Canadian male earned $3,400 a year. He put this money toward the East Side house that he still lives in over sixty years later. He soon worked his way up to games manager and spent most of his time walking around the park with a cigar in his mouth, "straightening out problems so everyone left the fair happy." He told me he was good at his job because "God gave me enough brains to talk to straighten things out."

Although Isaac talks openly about his friendships with gangsters, he is a man moved by others. He recalls seeing a girl in a wheelchair being pushed by her mother on the midway. He approached them and did what he could to make their day special. Here is how Isaac describes it:

Isaac working the crown and anchor wheel.
COURTESY OF ISAAC MESSINGER.

A woman was walking down the midway with a little girl. She was paralyzed. I see them walk and I talk to them. I used to smoke a cigar when I was younger. She says, "My little girl is paralyzed."

I say, "Come with me." I took her to the booth ... I could give anything I wanted and mark it down to the company, so I say, "Come with me and I get you something for the little girl."

So, we went to the booth there and the mother says, "What kind of teddy bear do you want?"

She says, "Give me this one"—she picked a white little teddy bear, you know. So, I say to the guy, "Give her the teddy bear." And they went home, and she thank me, and she had tears in her eyes. I still can remember this.

She phoned up and she asked for the boss. She says, "I'm phoning in because I was there with my little girl, and she's paralyzed a little bit, and you had a little guy working there with a cigar walking around. I want to tell you how nice of a person he is." I talk to them. I bought her some candy floss. I spend a little time.

At this point, Isaac begins to cry, then continues, "The years go by, and when you talk about it, it just breaks your heart."

While Isaac walked the park bringing joy to others, we were busy skimming money from our aprons in the bingo tent. Now, I realize that "everyone else is doing it" is not a proper defence for doing something wrong, but really—everyone else *was* doing it! In fact, one time I went into the back of the tent and saw Sam, my boss, counting out two giant stacks of bills. He took a quick glance around, somehow didn't see me, and then put one of the stacks directly into his pocket. Maybe it was legit, but it looked pretty shady. My dad shook his head and laughed when I told him about it. Many years later, when Sam turned sixty-five, he received a $40,000 retirement bonus from his work, which he spent in a few months. My dad asked Sam what he had done with the money, and he replied, "I blew it all on drugs and women." I suppose he might have meant beta blockers and dinner dates, but I suspect it was a lot more colourful than that.

When my interview with Isaac was wrapping up, he mentioned in passing that he was friends with former world heavyweight champion Rocky Marciano. He led me into a small room with the walls full of framed pictures of himself and various celebrities of the past. There were pictures of Isaac with Louis Armstrong, Mickey Rooney, Brenda Lee, and more. On one wall, he had an autographed picture of Rocky Marciano that said, "To Itzak, Keep Punching, Rocky Marciano." And right next to it was a picture of Isaac and Rocky together. I asked Isaac how he knew Rocky, and he told me:

I was friends with Rocky Marciano. He give me this picture and say, "You will remember me for the rest of your life, like I remember you—as a good friend." When he retired, we travelled together. He got invited to make speech. He used to take me with him. [He was a] very nice guy, good hearted, respected people. He was invited to parties to speak.

He used to take me with him, and they'd ask, "Who is the little guy with the cigar?"

Everybody want to know who I was, and [Rocky] would say, "He is just a friend of mine, you know, a good friend of mine."

I get the feeling that a lot of people consider Isaac a good friend. He may have been hired to return a favour, but they couldn't have found a better person for the job. This little streetwise cigar-smoking Polish immigrant made the PNE a better place to be. I'm glad he's still living in his very own "PNE prize home."

Isaac (left) with Rocky Marciano.
COURTESY OF ISAAC MESSINGER.

CHAPTER 8

Miss PNE

WHEN, IN 1989, Christine Weber was crowned Miss PNE at seventeen years old, one of her main duties was to be seen at the side of Erwin Swangard, the president of the PNE. Christine had to wear her crown and Miss PNE sash as the two walked around the grounds, flanked by four security guards. Although she describes "Mister Swangard" as gracious and kind, she also admits that she felt a bit like a trophy. After all, at eighty-one years old, Swangard was more than six decades her senior. She was also required to sit with him at all PNE Board meetings throughout the year—while still wearing her crown and sash. She listened, in her beauty queen accoutrements, as the board discussed upgrading electrical lines or streamlining parking regulations, and wondered, What am I doing here? Surely, there must have been other board members also questioning why Swangard kept the teen at his side during these meetings. I assume he did simply because he could; some old men love to be around young women.

There were other expectations and restrictions put on Christine as Miss PNE. For example, she was not allowed to be seen eating any food with her hands, including any teen staples like hamburgers, pizza, or potato chips. She had to wear a skirt or a dress whenever she was in public. And when she was at an event representing the PNE, she had a chaperone and a curfew. Along with these expectations came prizes. She won $2,000, a set of encyclopedias, and a lifetime pass to Playland, including parking. In the 1960s, pageant winners were also awarded driving lessons, which seems a bit condescending considering that at the time, the fair featured the Monkey Drome, a "monkey speedway" attraction that literally had monkeys driving cars around an oval track.

Although Christine now questions some of the things she had to do as Miss PNE, her overall experience was a positive one. Her beauty queen status gave her opportunities to travel and to meet people that she wouldn't have had otherwise, like the Governor General. However, the other Miss PNE contestants of the past may have had

The award-winning photo of Christine Weber's reaction to winning the 1989 Miss PNE contest.
PHOTO BY CRAIG HODGE / PNE.

a different experience. Between 1948 and the mid-1960s, winners of the Miss PNE contest routinely had their chest, waist, and hip measurements printed in the *Vancouver Sun* and *The Province*. The contestants' weight was published in the papers until the '80s. The 1955 winner, an eighteen-year-old, was described on the front page of the *Vancouver Sun* as weighing "127 well-distributed pounds."[17] In 1964, the same newspaper stated that that year's seventeen-year-old winner "stands five feet five inches, weighs 122 pounds, and her vital statistics are 36-24-36."[18] Forget about heart rate, blood pressure, and temperature—an hourglass figure was the way to check someone's vitals. (I'm not a doctor, but it seems like a waste of time for a paramedic to measure someone's breasts and hips.)

The contest entrants represented cities and small towns from all over the province vying for what was essentially a "Miss British Columbia" crown. Although the girls were not judged solely on their appearance, their looks were what got them in the door. Here is a breakdown of criteria from a 1957 article in the *Vancouver Sun*: "Contestants were judged 30 percent for charm, personality, and deportment, 30 percent for beauty of face and figure, 20 percent for ability to speak in public, and 20 percent for general intelligence and special ability."[19] It feels like the organizers went out of their way to say that looks were more important than intelligence. How hard would it have been to just make each of the four categories worth 25 percent? Also, "general intelligence" seems more like a requirement for an ex-con to qualify for independent living than a category in a beauty contest.

Of the forty-four winners in the pageant's history, forty-two of them were white. Nina Hamilton, who was of Cree, Shuswap Nation, and Scottish descent, broke the nineteen-year streak in 1967. And, in 1981, Devi Brar was the first and only Miss PNE of South Asian descent. Other than that, they were all white, which isn't really surprising. Many non-white Canadians didn't even have the right to

Nina Hamilton, Miss PNE 1967, with a guy in a Speedo.
CITY OF VANCOUVER ARCHIVES 180-4720.2.

vote for their government until the middle of the twentieth century, let alone choose the best-looking teen in a fairground pageant.

Christine saw her role as a "marketing tool for the province." While her classmates were going to parties or drinking in parks like normal teenagers, Christine would be sitting at a gala event with a group of foreign dignitaries and the premier of the province. She was often asked to speak to the crowd without time to prepare. She says, "I enjoyed it because I felt like it challenged me. I felt myself growing. I felt myself learning. And I knew that these skills would be really useful to me down the road in the future. But it was restrictive. It was challenging." She says the experience helped her to speak confidently in public, to think on her feet, and to walk into a situation cold without panicking. She looks back fondly on her reign and describes it as "life changing."

The title came with several duties and expectations that kept Christine busy most weekends through her final year of high school. She often had to travel to events throughout British Columbia, Alberta, Washington, Oregon, and California, which made it impossible for her to get a regular job. She knew that the prize money she won from the pageant wouldn't be enough for her university tuition, so she asked if there was any work the PNE could offer her. Initially, they had her answering phones in the administration office, but she was soon moved to a trailer, where she was given the job of engraving plastic name tags for park employees. Christine recalls this job with a laugh. "I had this noisy, noisy machine, and I had to take the letters, and I had to place them in the little template. And I had to engrave all of these plastic name tags, and it was so dusty and so hot in a trailer with no air conditioning." Adding to her discomfort was the requirement for Christine to be dressed up for the job in case anyone might see Miss PNE entering or leaving the tiny trailer. It was a long way from dining with the Governor General or walking around the fairgrounds wearing a crown.

Although Christine is proud of her reign, it is not something she brings up much anymore. The people she works with don't know that she was once Miss PNE. "I don't generally talk about it. Not that I don't want to. I'm not hiding it. But I feel like people get the wrong impression of me when they find out that I used to be in pageants, because in their mind, they're thinking *Toddlers & Tiaras*." She went into drafting in university and now works as a senior interior designer. She explains, "I design interiors for everything to do with elders. Everything from luxury independent living, assisted living, hospitals, and health care design." In contrast to the common stereotype of the shallow beauty queen, Christine says that most of the contestants were motivated high achievers who saw the pageant as a stepping stone.

Another former Miss PNE, Gloria Macarenko, went on to become an award-winning journalist for the CBC and is a recipient of the Order of Canada. When I spoke to Gloria about her experience with the pageant, she was more excited to talk about the public speaking opportunities it gave her than the beauty queen status. She described the contest as "that line between a real beauty pageant and a farm fair" and claims she never saw herself as the pageant type.

Gloria grew up in Prince Rupert, and the very first time she ever went to the PNE was in 1978, when she was crowned Miss PNE at the age of seventeen:

> My parents and I would come down for our summer holiday and drive through Vancouver on our way to visit relatives on Vancouver Island. And as soon as we'd come by the PNE ... we had a little truck and camper, and I'd be nose up to the window, kind of looking [and asking], "Can we stop, Dad? Can we stop when you see the roller coaster?" And [he] was like, "No, we're not stopping. We're going right through. We've got to catch the ferry to the Island." So, I had never been to the PNE. Ever.

She arrived at the pageant with low expectations, just happy to be part of it, and admits to feeling like "the country girl in the city." In just a couple of days, her life was changed when she was crowned the winner. A caption accompanying her picture in *The Province* reads, "seventeen-year-old Gloria Macarenko from Prince Rupert has won the PNE pageant for 1978. The young brunette won a trophy, $1,000, a professional modelling course, a gold lifetime pass to Playland, and a kiss from Premier Bennett."[20] Another perk of winning was an upgrade to a suite in the Hotel Vancouver. Gloria was joined in the room by her mom, aunt, and sister, who had been staying in a motel during the pageant. "We were like the Beverly Hillbillies in the hotel. So, it was really fun."

Gloria Macarenko, Miss PNE 1978, with a crew from the demolition derby.
PHOTO BY CROTON STUDIO.

Like Christine Weber, Gloria Macarenko sees her experience as positive and important step in her career. She was already planning on a career in journalism before she won, and the public speaking duties of being Miss PNE helped her achieve a comfort level with crowds. She worked at a local radio station in Prince Rupert during her Grade 12 year and would often have to fly to different events as Miss PNE on the weekends. Gloria developed a close relationship with PNE president Erwin Swangard and his wife, Doris, during this year, continuing into her time at journalism school after her reign as Miss PNE ended.

> Erwin, in his capacity as former managing editor of the *Vancouver Sun*, took me under his wing as a journalist, and we would have some great conversations about the state of journalism. I spent a lot of time with him and his wife. My father had died when I was just thirteen. [Erwin] had three sons but didn't have any daughters. So, he kind of took me under his wing as a father figure as well. And so, I felt very, very fortunate that I had him and Doris in my life.

I asked Gloria if she was ever uncomfortable with Swangard's attention, and she said, "You know, I guess I always felt I had something to say, so I never felt like just the person with the crown and the sash. So I just never acquiesced to that kind of a role, and I think nobody saw me like that, and I didn't see myself like that." Both Gloria and Christine see past the stereotypical parts of the pageant to the valuable life experience they gained during their time as Miss PNE.

Looking back, Christine says, "The physical part of it—I never agreed with that. I never thought that was okay. I felt very uncomfortable, being judged on my body or on the way I walked, but I understood the rest of it. I understood that as a Miss PNE, you are a marketing tool. You are part of the machine to promote the PNE and to promote the province." The PNE has since found ways to promote itself without relying on the bodies of high school girls. However, it's not surprising that these beauty queens played a large part in the marketing of the PNE. From the carnival games to the rides to the food stands, the overwhelming majority of employees were teenagers. The pageant contestants were just another group of teens working for the fair. The only difference was that Miss PNE had to eat her minidonuts with a knife and fork.

Christine Weber, Miss PNE 1989.
PHOTO BY CRAIG HODGE / PNE.

The Small of Rome

Since a large number of PNE employees were East Side kids of Italian descent, like me, I offer you this view from our perspective.

I HAVE OFTEN HEARD the phrase "he peaked in high school" used as a put-down. It implies that someone's best days are behind them, that they only flourished in a small pond and were unable to adapt to the larger world. This is usually perpetuated by people who hated high school, people who are still angry about their experience. But really, how many people actually peak at all? Most people ride out a plateau, then retroactively assign peaks and valleys to their lives to imply dramatic context. If you did peak in high school, you shouldn't be ashamed. It's better to have peaked when you were young than to never have peaked at all. And really, what kind of an asshole walks around in their twenties or thirties saying they are peaking? Now, don't get me wrong, I'm not laying all this groundwork so I can admit that *I* peaked in high school. Not at all. You see, my background—like many kids with roots in East Vancouver—is 100 percent Italian, which means, of course, that I peaked in elementary school.

I didn't realize it at the time, but my peak coincided with puberty. Specifically, I was going through it before all the non-Italian kids my age, which gave me a one- or two-year advantage over my peers. This also happened to be when I was at my best in sports. All of a sudden, I could run right over other kids in lacrosse; their prepubescent bodies crumpled under my hulking five-foot-five frame. At twelve years old, I was already as tall as my parents. Who knew where it would end? (Turns out five-six is where it ended.) And the tiny bit of muscle I gained was accompanied by a tiny bit of hair on my upper lip, which gave me more than a tiny bit of confidence, especially around girls.

For most twelve-year-old boys of Italian heritage in Vancouver, the future looks bright. Kids with names like Tony, Franco, and Claudio dominate soccer games on elementary playgrounds. We all look back on our school days and remember some swarthy kid who just seemed bigger, faster, and stronger than everyone else. Unfortunately, every-thing changes by about Grade 8 or 9, when the other kids start going through puberty too. The only thing that doesn't really change for little Italian guys, however, is our belief that we are big. Because our self-image was created at such an influential age, it's almost impossible to reconfigure. That's why I don't agree with the common belief that a lot of little Italian men have "small man syndrome." You must actually know that you are small in order to try to compensate for it. Short Italian men don't know they're small. That's why we walk around with a disproportionate amount of confidence. We decided at the age of twelve that we were big, and we never looked back. We assumed we would be stars—athletes, performers—getting into limos and seeing the world. Instead, we climb in and out of vans that say things like "Cuzetto Plumbing" or "Ugo and Joe's Meat Market" on the side. So, the next time you see a little Italian man wandering around the city in a blue track suit, looking confused and a little angry, try to show some compassion. After all, this is not the world we were promised. Our popularity has the shelf life of minidonuts: hot one minute, a greasy bag of dough the next.

Me trying very hard to be cool when I was twelve.
COURTESY OF NICK MARINO.

CHAPTER 9

Looking Up

EVERY YEAR, from 1910 up until 1995, families lined the Vancouver streets to get a glimpse of the floats, community groups, and convertible cars of the PNE Parade. My sister loved to go, but I never liked parades. I always felt like we were waiting for a show that never actually started, forced instead to watch floats advertising local businesses and uninterested Cub Scout troops marching out of time. In the 1940s, there was another much smaller parade on the PNE grounds that would have held my attention as a kid, though I understand why it no longer exists. A show called Henry Kramer's Midget Parade snaked its way through the Gayway at the PNE to draw attention to the sideshows or, as they were commonly called back then, the "freak shows." (This derogatory term for little people has fallen so far out of favour that in 2020, even Hockey Canada stopped using it to refer to players aged sixteen to eighteen.) The PNE had a Freak Auditorium that featured performers ranging from fat ladies to a man with alligator skin, and everything in between. Some of the acts were clearly fakes—a few of the little people were obviously children, the four-legged lady never stood up and walked around, and the headless woman almost certainly had a head. The fat lady seemed to be as advertised, though. There is even an article from 1959 in which her

This terrifying float was featured in the PNE Parade for a few years in the 1940s and '50s.
CITY OF VANCOUVER ARCHIVES 180-1548.

husband reassures audiences that her recent fifteen-pound weight loss is not noticeable on her 537-pound frame. Another article from that same year claims, "The midway freak show is well worth the price of admission. Two of the acts, the armless girl and the sheep-headed men, are rated by independent showmen as the best in the world."[21] It seems odd to be the best at not having arms. And how many other "sheep-headed" men were out there to compare with these ones?

Eko and Iko, the Sheep-Headed Men, were sometimes billed as the Monkey Men, the Missing Links, or the Martians. In reality, they were George and Willie Muse, African American brothers with albinism. Their story is bizarre and horrifying. As children, they were reportedly kidnapped from a tobacco farm in Virginia by a "freak hunter" who lured them with candy and forced them to work

The four-legged woman at the Freak Auditorium in 1941.
CITY OF VANCOUVER ARCHIVES 180-1034.

in sideshows throughout the southern United States. Some reports suggest that their mother may have allowed them to perform at the circus for a couple of months, but they were never returned. Either way, they were told that their mother was dead, and they lived as underpaid, exploited captives for decades. When the circus returned to their hometown in 1927, their mother, who had been trying to track them down for years, was able to convince police at the show that the brothers were being held against their will. She hired a lawyer, who freed them from an unfair "contract" with the Ringling Brothers Circus. In time, however, the brothers found that the only way to support themselves was to continue to work as sideshow performers. George and Willie were treated somewhat better upon their return and were able to send some money home to their mother. They worked into their midsixties, which was when they performed at the PNE as the Sheep-Headed Men. Their mother used the money they sent to her to buy a small piece of property where the brothers lived after they retired. George died at the age of eighty-two, and Willie lived to the incredible age of 108. He claimed to have hated only one person in his life: James Herman "Candy" Shelton, the man who allegedly kidnapped the brothers and put them on display. When Willie was feeling generous, he would refer to Shelton as the "scum of the Earth," other times simply calling him a "cocksucker."[22]

I assume we can all agree that freak shows have no place in modern society, but through much of the last century, the public accepted them. Not only did the performers find work at fairs and exhibitions, they also performed throughout the rest of the year. Henry Kramer's little people performers also worked at the Cave nightclub in Vancouver. What surprises me most is that freak shows continued into the 1970s, when my parents were bringing our family to the PNE. I have no memory of seeing these tents, but I have seen pictures to prove that they were there in my lifetime. The demise of the freak show was predicted in a 1959 *Province* article that opens with the line, "Medical science is killing the freak show."[23] The writer details how advances in medicine are threatening the supply of future "freaks." There is also an advice column from 1940 that helps a mother deal with their child's fear of "people with bodily imperfections." The columnist suggests letting the child put on their own freak show, dressing up as a fat lady or some other "freak" to help create an "unterrifying familiarity with

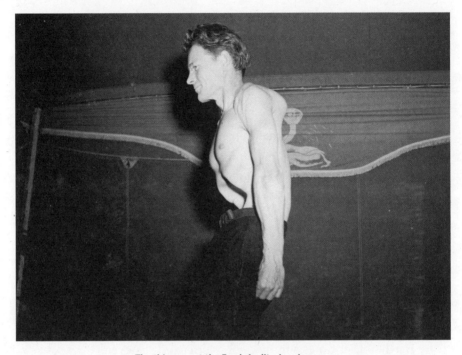

The thin man at the Freak Auditorium in 1940.
CITY OF VANCOUVER ARCHIVES 180-1024.

personal differences."[24] I hope no one asked her advice on how to get comfortable around people from other cultures. Sideshow performers were just a small part of the entertainment at the fair, however. There have been hundreds of different types of shows and events at the PNE since its inception, and the fair has done an excellent job of programming top-tier performers, including Elvis Presley, the Beatles, and Johnny Cash. There was also something called "Celebrity Milking," which could mean a couple of different things but seems gross either way.

Some of the daily events and exhibitions of the mid-twentieth century sound a bit strange now. One of the sideshow tents included a photographic display called "Girls Ruined by Dope." A trailer held a reconstruction of the Saint Valentine's Day Massacre in waxed figures, fake blood, and actual bricks from the murder site where seven gangsters were gunned down. Apparently, the polio exhibit was very popular with children, as were the free chest X-rays in the tuberculosis tent. And in 1941, the Freckle Face Championship was held. Here is how it was advertised in the *Vancouver Sun*:

> Freckled, and proud of it! That's what they are, these sporty youngsters who have gone through the ordeal of having their freckles counted in public. In fact, they just love being freckled—if they can only win that bicycle! And now they're going to count them again, for the last time, to see who really is the "most freckledest" face in all Greater Vancouver and New Westminster. Roll up, folks. It's going to be FUN![25]

If anything, this contest proves that we all have different definitions of fun.

The fair has always looked for ways to get attention, and in the late 1960s, it tried to take advantage of the public's fascination with space travel by adding the hundred-metre(330-foot)-high Space Tower attraction. At a time when David Bowie sang about a "Space Oddity" and Steve Miller claimed to be a "space cowboy," the world was looking to the sky, and the PNE followed. The Space Tower gave sixty people a slow, revolving ride to the height of sixty-five metres (216 feet). It made money for a few years, then struggled to stay out of the red for most of the decade before being dismantled in 1979. By all accounts, it was a little boring. I remember it being one of the attractions my mom didn't want to waste money on. The Sky Glider, another attraction with a spacey name, was a much more popular and successful ride. It was a two-seat open-air gondola that ran from one end of the park to the other. Riders would cover 442 metres (1,450 feet) in seven minutes as they cruised above the crowds at heights of about twelve metres (forty feet). It was a great way to get an overview of the entire fair. The Sky Glider had two stations, one

Like the Freckle Face Championship and the freak show,
the ladies' nail-driving contest is no longer part of the fair.
CITY OF VANCOUVER ARCHIVES 180-6102.

at the entrance to the park off Hastings Street, near the roller coaster, and the other one by the Showmart building, toward Renfrew Street.

The Sky Glider did not have a lock on the safety bar that was pulled down before you left the station, which always made me a bit uncomfortable as a kid. But for some people, that wasn't the scariest part of the ride. There were always kids who couldn't resist throwing stuff on the people below as they rode above the midway. Fairgoers under the path of the Sky Glider were showered with spit, soft drinks, carnival treats, and loose change. The ride moved slowly enough that a person who got hit could easily identify who had done it and have time to walk down to the exit to confront the troublemaker. "I'll see you at the end!" was a common threat yelled up to offending riders.

I remember hearing my cousin's friend tell a story about some teens who poured a drink on him, so he waited for them at the end and then beat the shit out of them. I particularly remember him saying that he gave them the "shoe factory," which was his way of saying he kicked them. A lot.

When my wife, Jeanne, was twelve, she had a scary incident on the Sky Glider when her fourteen-year-old cousin poured a drink on a group of teenage boys below them. One of the guys yelled, "I'm gonna fucking kill you!" Jeanne, who hadn't been involved in the pouring, had to wait in the gondola like a sitting duck, hoping she wouldn't be attacked when they arrived at the end. The girls took off in a sprint

The Space Tower took riders sixty-five metres (216 feet) up above the fairgrounds.
CITY OF VANCOUVER ARCHIVES 180-4028.04.

The Sky Glider, high above an all-terrain vehicle show during the fair in 1971.
CITY OF VANCOUVER ARCHIVES 180-6879.

as soon as they reached the station and were somehow able to lose the boys in the crowd. Incidents like these were much scarier than a restraint that didn't lock.

There was a lot to see on the seven-minute ride, including, if you looked north, the demolition derby. For many kids of the seventies, the demolition derby was the highlight of the fair. Watching these fearless drivers crash their cars into each other in a motorized battle royale was hilarious and exhilarating. And somehow, in all this mayhem, no one ever got seriously injured, unless you consider split helmets and concussions serious—but hey, it was the 1970s. There was even an instance of the police having to step in right after the event. A tow truck driver named Murray Chambers was told he could pick up an old car to use at the derby. Unfortunately, he towed away the wrong one, a car that was identical to the one he was supposed to take. And here is where the story gets strange: when Chambers used the car in

The demolition derby was the highlight of the fair for me.
CITY OF VANCOUVER ARCHIVES 180-3857.

a demolition derby event at the PNE, the owner happened to be in the audience, watching his missing car being reduced to a sputtering, smoky heap of scrap metal. The owner informed police about the stolen car and pointed it out during the event. They waited until the derby was over and then immediately arrested Chambers.

The Sky Glider would also take you over the midway, which included a long section of food stands that defined the fair experience for a lot of visitors. The blatant capitalism of a carnival feels like just the right place for some of the things that have come and gone over the years. Take, for example, the introduction of horseburgers to the fair in 1951. The front page of the *Vancouver Sun* had the headline "Fairgoers Jump to Horse" above a picture of two men who looked unnecessarily excited to be eating grilled nag. Apparently, the attraction was the cost; you could buy a horseburger for twenty cents, while hamburgers went for as much as thirty-five cents. The caption under the picture says, "How to get even with horses that don't win at nearby Exhibition Park racetrack is demonstrated at the PNE horseburger stand ... Theory is—if you can't beat 'em, eat 'em."[26] Another option might be to stop gambling on horses, if it leaves you seeking revenge. The horseburger never became a staple at the fair, but the idea of a low-cost burger remained. John Ronning, father of former Canuck Cliff Ronning, told me, "They had a place where you could get an onion burger for fifteen cents. It was just onions inside it. If you wanted hamburger meat in it, it would cost you twenty-five cents." Sounds better than eating a horse, but the onion burger also failed to become a regular food at the fair.

In recent years, bizarre food is one of the ways the fair has been able to make headlines. In much the same way that performers at the freak show were used to draw attention to the PNE, strange food combinations like squid-ink corn dogs, macaroni-and-cheese-flavoured ice cream, and noodles served on cotton candy are featured in a 2022 article about the fair. This is a relatively recent development, however. For decades, standard fair food like hamburgers, mini-donuts, the occasional "ethnic" food stand, and some free samples were enough to excite the public. A *Vancouver Sun* article about food at the fair in 1996 includes this line: "Apart from a few engaging oddities (the wildly exotic Pearl Milk Tea with tapioca at Sam's Desserts, for one), the food building now offers pretty much what you'd find in the average mall food court and none of it is free."[27] Bubble tea has become so common in the city that it's weird to think it was ever considered an "oddity." But that is the trajectory of some foods, like pizza. My dad told me that in the early 1950s, you couldn't get pizza in Vancouver. The first time he tasted it was in New York,

A young couple eating a foot-long hot dog, *Lady and the Tramp* style.
CITY OF VANCOUVER ARCHIVES 180-2219.

when he was on his way to Italy with his mom in 1952. The first pizza available in Vancouver was actually at the PNE. Local restauranteur Tevie Smith sold slices at the fair in 1955. He explains in a *Vancouver Sun* article it wasn't exactly an instant success: "You know where the Coliseum is, well, that was a roller coaster called the Giant Dipper. I sold pissa—because they didn't even know what to call it—at the roller coaster for nineteen cents a slice. And believe me, they took a bite out of it and then threw it at me. They didn't want to eat that [stuff]. I used to chase them down the midway."[28]

You can't talk about the food at the PNE without mentioning Hunky Bill's, a perogy stand owned by Bill Konyk that has been at the fair since 1967. Konyk was so successful at the PNE that he branched out and opened several restaurants across the Lower Mainland.

I remember seeing my mom laugh and shake her head as she read an article in 1980 that claimed the name "Hunky Bill's" was racist. Apparently *hunky* was a slur for Ukrainians, a shortened version of *bohunk*, and Konyk was being pressured by other Ukrainians to change the name of his business. I have to admit, Ukrainian slurs were and still are out of the range of my knowledge of racial slurs, but I will take it as read that being called "hunky" is a bad thing to some people. Konyk argued that he was basically reclaiming the word and making it positive. Kind of like the Ukrainian N-word, I guess. The article includes a letter from an offended Ukrainian Canadian.

> What would be the reaction of the Italian, Chinese or Jewish community to establishment names such "Tony the Wop's Pizza Hut" or "Chinky Lee's Laundry" or "Kike's Corned Beef Sandwiches"? These fictitious names are not a far cry from "Hunky Bill's Ukrainian Sausage."[29]

It seems like two of them *are* a far cry from "Hunky" to me. It reminds you that not all slurs are created equal. Also, why didn't the Jewish one get a name like Tony and Lee did? (And, for the record, I'd happily eat at Tony the Wop's.) The Ukrainian Canadian Professional and Business Association of Vancouver eventually filed a complaint under the BC Human Rights Code in 1980. They said that the name Hunky Bill's "was an affront to the dignity of persons of Ukrainian descent." Konyk won the case in Supreme Court in 1983 and continued to use the name until he died in 2019.[30]

Food is the biggest attraction for some, but for others, the rides are their reason to visit the fair. I used to love seeing all the other rides as I floated above on the Sky Glider. Some of them are still there, but lots are gone. There was the Haunted House, the Tilt-A-Whirl, the Giant Octopus, the Music Express, the Super Loops, the Scooters, and the Wave Swinger, among many others. The Wild Mouse always scared the shit out of me because it was so rickety that I assumed Playland wasn't putting enough money into keeping it properly maintained. I'm sure they were, but something about that single-car roller coaster felt like it was about to collapse in a rusty heap or like the cars were going to fly right off the edge. I assume that was the point, but it is a different kind of rush than you get at a place like Disneyland, where the thrill is based more on physics than economics.

I remember the excitement and the huge lineups when they added the Pirate Ship ride in 1984. Here is how the PNE website describes the ride: "The pendulum like motion of the ride provides Buccaneers a feeling of complete weightlessness as the boat hangs at the height of the swing prior to changing direction. You'll definitely need to find your 'land legs' after this ride!"[31] The Pirate Ship was and is a very popular ride, and there are two things I always think about when I see it. More than anything, I remember the long-haired, sunglasses-wearing ride attendant standing on the platform, his back to the ride as it rushed by him so close that I feared he would be struck by the hull of the ship and launched over the gambling tents into the demolition derby. He would sometimes smack the ride with his hand as it swung by, his stoic expression never changing, his long hair blowing around his face from the force of the ship. I loved the juxtaposition of his rehearsed cool with the panicked and screaming riders swinging back and forth behind him. It wasn't always cool for everyone on the ride, though. The other thing I think about is how a security guard from the fair told me that the Pirate Ship had malfunctioned one time in the 1990s, and the workers were unable to stop it for over half an hour. The people on it had pleaded to be let off as the inside of the ship turned into a sloshing vomitorium.

All amusement parks have issues with their rides, and Playland at the PNE is no different. However, as far as I can tell, there have been very few injuries. A couple of people have died, but it was not the fault of the PNE at all. In the early days of the Giant Dipper roller coaster, a sixteen-year-old tried to impress his friends by attempting a handstand on the safety bar while the roller coaster was in motion. He slipped and fell to his death. And in 1985, a twenty-six-year-old climbed one of the towers that held up the Sky Glider. He jumped onto a passing gondola chair but could only hold on for a few seconds before plummeting twelve metres (forty feet) to the concrete. He was rushed to the hospital, where he died later that day.

There was one accident on a ride that I personally remember as I was working when it happened. It was my first year at the fair, when I was blowing up balloons, and the Jet Star 2 was one of the newest rides in the park. It was a single-car roller coaster that sat four people at a time and boasted speeds of up to ninety kilometres (fifty-six miles) per hour. There were no seat belts or restraints on the ride, but the cars were well padded. On August 25, 1980, Playland experienced a power failure when several of the larger rides started at the exact same time. There was a double braking system in place to deal with power outages, but it failed on one of the Jet Star's cars. Here is how the mother of two of the girls in the car described what she saw to a *Vancouver Sun* reporter:

> I was petrified. All I could think about was the car flying off the track. It was almost up to the top, more than halfway up, when it stopped. Everything was quiet for a couple of seconds, then it went all the way backwards and slammed into the stationary car behind it. My youngest daughter was sitting in the back, and she got the full force of it ... there's no way I'd let my kids go on that ride again.[32]

Her daughter spent the night in the hospital and was released the next day with a badly bruised back. Provincial inspectors reported that the accident was due to a film of oil between the brake drum and the shoe. The malfunctioning car was taken out of rotation, and the ride was soon back in service.

The Sky Glider in 1971, a year after it opened.
CITY OF VANCOUVER ARCHIVES 180-6891.

The Sky Glider was taken down in 1985 and never replaced. The dream of space travel was no longer in the zeitgeist and for a while, the PNE stopped looking skyward. The late 1980s and early '90s saw a lot of local hostility toward the PNE, ultimately leading to the unfulfilled promise to convert it entirely to green space. Eventually, though, the PNE would look up again, adding both the Hellevator and the Revelation in 2000, two rides that briefly caused an uproar with some Christians. Early promos for the Revelation included the slogan "The Second Coming," and a TV ad showed a turnstile clicking to 666—this prompted some churchgoers to suggest boycotting the PNE. Both rides were successful and added much-needed height to the amusement park. The Revelation rotates on a forty-nine-metre (160-foot) arm and spins riders at speeds over a hundred kilometres (sixty-two miles) per hour, while the Hellevator propels patrons at seventy-five kilometres (forty-six miles) per hour to a height of sixty-two metres (202 feet).

And in 2011, a spinning swing ride called the Atmosfear opened. It takes riders sixty-six metres (218 feet) up in the air and swings them around at seventy-five kilometres (forty-seven miles) per hour, making it over half a metre (two feet) higher than the experience on the Space Tower and more than ten times faster. Although the PNE may seem like it has remained constant, many attractions, rides, and snacks have come and gone. But whether you are eating a horseburger or a squid-ink corn dog, whether you are cheering on the drivers in the demolition derby or applauding the SuperDogs, you are experiencing your generation's version of the same thing that came before. It is surprising how much the PNE has changed over the years, only to remain the same.

CHAPTER 10

Bobby and Lui

ALTHOUGH CLELIA LENARDUZZI had three sons on the Vancouver Whitecaps in 1978, she was too nervous to attend the games for fear of seeing them get injured. Instead, she would sit on the back porch of the family house a half a block from the PNE grounds and listen for the roar of the crowd coming from Empire Stadium to gauge how her boys were doing. She would have to wait until the boys came home after the game to hear the whole story. Her husband, Giovanni, never missed the opportunity to watch his sons play, however, and enjoyed the twelve-minute walk from his house on Dundas Street to the stadium. On August 3, 1978, Giovanni was among the 24,000 fans who watched three of his sons—Sam, Bob, and Dan—play in the same professional soccer game. The Whitecaps won the game by a score of 6–0, and Bob scored two goals. Mrs. Lenarduzzi heard a lot of cheering that night, as the crowd went wild for the six goals and also gave the team four separate standing ovations.

Bob, or Bobby, Lenarduzzi was voted North American Player of the Year in 1978 and was an instrumental part of the Vancouver Whitecaps soccer team that won the championship a year later. He holds the record for most games ever played in the North American Soccer League and somehow managed to play all eleven

Bob Lenarduzzi at Empire Stadium in 1979.
PHOTO BY KENT KALLBERG, COURTESY OF THE BC SPORTS HALL OF FAME.

positions, including goalie, during his time on the team. He joined the Whitecaps for their first season in 1974 and never looked back. Many outstanding players have worn Whitecaps jerseys over the years, including Alphonso Davies, Kevin Hector, and Peter Beardsley, but the through line in Vancouver soccer is Bob Lenarduzzi. As well as playing for the Whitecaps in their NASL glory days, he coached the Vancouver 86ers to four national titles and served as president of Whitecaps FC in Major League Soccer for several years. Playing for a hometown team was a dream for Bob. "Had I known back then that I'd spend the majority of my career in Vancouver, I would have been absolutely ecstatic," he is quoted saying on the Whitecaps official website.[33] I can't think of a more East Van sports story than the local Italian boy who becomes an integral part of his hometown team at a stadium he can walk to from his family home. Oddly enough, that story could apply to more than just Bob.

Lui Passaglia, who is one year older than Bob, holds the record for most points scored by a professional football player in any league. He was the kicker for the BC Lions for twenty-five seasons, and, like Bob, grew up a few blocks from the PNE and Empire Stadium, where he started his professional career. I never followed football that closely, but I was always aware of Lui. After all, he played for the BC Lions from the time I was eight until I was thirty-three. Or, to put it another way, I gained approximately 150 pounds over the course of Lui's career, though I don't think those two things are related. Lui won three Grey Cups with the Lions, was voted the Grey Cup's Most Valuable Canadian twice, and was a CFL All-Star on several occasions. Although he made his mark in the Canadian Football League as a kicker, he managed to score two touchdowns in his career—one in his first game, in 1976, and one in his last, in 2000. I asked Lui how he managed to carve out such a long career for himself, and he said:

I felt like that kid in the east end of Vancouver. I always felt like when I was playing, I was playing as that kid ... When I joined the Lions, playing all those years, I was that kid in the east end going to Empire Stadium or going to a hockey game and saying, Hey, one day I'm gonna be out there in front of these crowds, showing them what I can do. I was lucky. I got lucky and found a niche and found a place that wanted me for that long, and I'm very grateful [to have grown] up in the east end of Vancouver.

Bob echoed these comments when I asked him about growing up a half a block from the PNE: "I never ever thought anything other than that this is the best place to live. If you had to choose someplace to live, I would have chosen there. You've got the fair, you've got a soccer pitch. It was fantastic." That soccer pitch, Callister Park, played an important role in both Bob's and Lui's lives.

I mentioned to Lui that my family was more into soccer than football, and he said his family was the same, that every Sunday they would go to Callister Park to watch teams in the Pacific Coast League. For Bob, Callister Park was everything. "Callister was my Wembley. I was there every weekend, and I actually got a job out of it as well, because I was a ball boy at Callister Park." He recalls dodging traffic on Renfrew Street to retrieve balls and chasing people who tried to take the ones that were kicked out of the park. And when they weren't chasing errant balls, the boys would become the halftime show. Some of Bob's fondest memories of Callister Park were when the three ball boys would take turns shooting on each other between the first and second half. The audience would cheer them on as they tried to score in front of the packed house of up to five thousand people. It was not the most modern facility, and Bob says that "in the heat of summer, if a match had been lit and dropped, [the stadium] would have gone up in flames."

Lui Passaglia.

Both Bob and Lui told me about having the chance to dress for a men's game at the stadium when they were teenagers. They both wore the Columbus uniform, the team started by and for the Italians in the community. Lui dressed but never left the bench. Bob, at thirteen years old, was put in for the last ten minutes of a game. He has one distinct memory of that experience: "All I can remember is getting walloped by some guy who just shoulder-charged me and knocked me on my ass. I remember looking up and seeing blue sky. That was my initiation to Callister." As professional athletes, Bob and Lui wore different uniforms, but, coincidentally, were both number 5.

Callister was just one part of the neighbourhood that Bob and Lui roamed as kids, both spending most of their free time playing sports. Sometimes Bob and his friends would take a hockey net to one of the parking lots on the PNE grounds and play hockey for the day. Lui spent a lot of his time at Hastings Elementary School, two blocks from the PNE grounds, playing hockey, soccer, and football with friends. He would also go there alone to kick field goals and dream of being a pro. "I used to show up at Hastings Elementary School, by myself a lot of times, on the gravel field, and just kick footballs over soccer goalposts and pretend to be Ted Gerela or Roy Gerela." The Gerelas, from Powell River, were both professional kickers—Roy won a Super Bowl with the Pittsburgh Steelers, and Ted played for the BC Lions.

As well as playing sports in and around the PNE grounds, Bob and Lui were able to walk over to Empire Stadium or an adjoining practice field to watch their heroes practising. In the late 1960s, the city had a professional soccer team called the Vancouver Royals who played at Empire Stadium. They were managed by Frenec Puskás, a Hungarian superstar considered to be one of the greatest soccer players of all time. When I asked Bob about the Royals, he said:

> I can vividly remember watching the Vancouver Royals practice in 1967. So, I would have been twelve years old, and I would walk over from my house ... And what I do remember is Puskás taking shots, warming the keeper up. And although he couldn't move, he was always a pretty big guy, but he would take shots on the goalie, and it wasn't really good for the goalie because he was just bending them

in the top corner, and the keeper was just taking them out of the back of the net.

Just seven years later, Bob would be playing professionally for his hometown team.

Lui would also walk down to watch practices, but he favoured the BC Lions. "I always looked forward to going there one way or the other, because the Lions were there. They were practising there in the old days, either on a side field there by the stadium or in the stadium itself. You know, you could go down there and catch a practice." He still appreciates all the opportunities that living close to the PNE gave to him. "It was a great neighborhood to grow up in, especially if you're into sports. So back in that day, you had the freedom to roam from one area to the other. You never worried about your children that much because the neighborhood kind of policed itself."

Although neither Bob nor Lui ever worked at the PNE, they both have stories that echo those of all the other locals who grew up in the area. Bob explains how he earned money during the fair at the ages of ten and eleven.

I never worked at PNE, but what I did was, I parked cars. [I used] our house, but we only had two spots. So, there was a guy on the same block, his name was George ... and he had a big backyard, no fence, so I could park about fourteen cars in there. So, my whole PNE time was parking cars, and I got a quarter a car, and he got seventy-five cents a car, which I thought at the time was good, but I probably should have negotiated a better deal. Anyway, I got a quarter per car, and I'd come home every night and throw all the quarters on the table, and over the course of that two weeks at the PNE, I'd make 150 bucks. [It was] a lot of money for me.

Lui remembers trying to find a way in without paying:

> I can let you know that I snuck into the PNE as a kid
> because I couldn't afford to get in at that time. I wasn't
> working, as a young kid. You try to find an angle of how
> to get into the fair and stuff. We had a bunch of kids that
> just for fun tried to see if we could get in. Sometimes
> it worked. Sometimes it didn't ... I remember as a kid
> trying, when the fair was on, with a couple other buddies,
> trying to get in [by] either asking somebody at the gate or
> finding a hole in the fence somewhere.

Bob and Lui both played youth soccer for Grandview Legion 179, though somehow they didn't know each other, despite living within blocks and being only a year apart in age. I like to think that their paths must have crossed at some point. They were both on teams that won the Sun Tournament of Champions, which was basically the provincial championship of soccer at the time. Bob was recruited by Reading FC in England and was playing abroad by the time he was fifteen years old. Lui focused on football and won three provincial high school championships with the Notre Dame Jugglers, where he played quarterback, safety, and punter. He went on to Simon Fraser University in Burnaby, BC, where he played quarterback, receiver, and kicker. Remarkably, Empire Stadium was the home field for his high school, university, and professional teams.

Both Bob and Lui have distinct memories of their first professional games for their hometown teams at Empire Stadium. Bob recalls how his parents were invited to the opening game of the Whitecaps' first season. It would be the only game his mom ever attended in person.

> [The owner] said, "We need to get your mom and dad
> out to the opening game." And they are not fancy people.
> So, he said, "[They're] going to sit in the Queen's Box

with me." And my mom was panicking right up until the game because it wasn't something that she was used to, nor my dad, for that matter ... It was halfway up, and it was a special area for VIPs. So, yeah, for the first game they were really not comfortable with it.

His mom would retreat to the safety of the back porch for the rest of Bob's time at Empire Stadium. Two years later, Lui would make his professional football debut on the same field.

Here is how he remembers it:

I think the one game that really kind of hit me was the first game I ever played there with the Lions. I dressed and I got to play in that game against Saskatchewan and Ronnie Lancaster, and it was pretty well a full house. I mean, we didn't play well. We lost, but I got to play and scored a touchdown. I never got a chance to kick a convert or field goal that game, but the feeling of coming out of that dressing room in that stadium where everybody, a lot of the past legends of soccer or football had come through and you always dreamed of doing the same thing, and here you are coming out of that tunnel as a professional athlete, it was a pretty humbling experience, but also one that, as you can tell, I've never forgotten.

Vancouver crowds were always good to Lui. During Lions games, it was common to hear the crowd chanting, "LOUUUUU!" as he lined up for a field goal. "If you're gonna play sports and you're a local kid, you couldn't have it any better than I did. Whether I was playing in East Vancouver at Empire Stadium or BC Place or travelling through the province, I was just very, very fortunate," says Lui. "The fact that I could go to a stadium and have fifty thousand people say

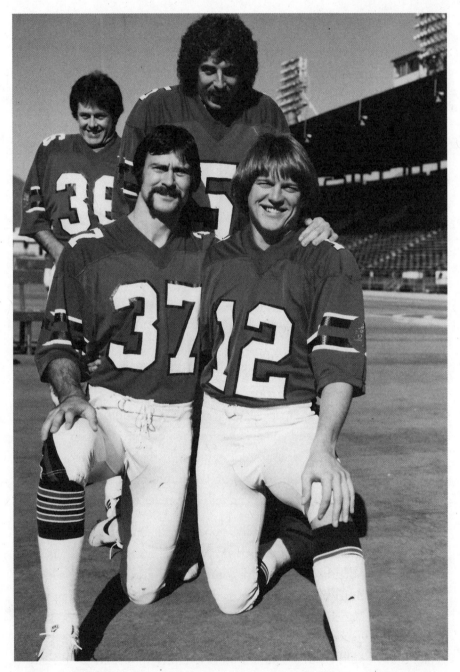

Lui Passaglia (back row, centre) with his BC Lions teammates in Empire Stadium in the mid-1970s.
COURTESY OF THE BC SPORTS HALL OF FAME.

'LOUUUUU!' every time I stepped on the field—that kind of put an exclamation mark on whether I made it or not."

Bob was also well received by the hometown fans. His good looks made him a hit with many female fans, including my wife, Jeanne, when she was younger. At fourteen, she waited in line with other excited teenage girls to get a kiss from Bob at the Whitecaps victory parade in downtown Vancouver, held the day after the they had won the 1979 Soccer Bowl. Thousands of people jammed the streets to get a glimpse of the returning heroes. Bob was one of the biggest sports figures in Vancouver at the time and would soon have a poster aimed at the female market. It was the type of poster that would not have looked out of place next to pictures of Shaun Cassidy, Leif Garrett, or John Travolta. Bob is the most important figure in Vancouver soccer, and I don't hold it against him that he kissed my wife. To be honest, I was such a huge Whitecaps fan at the time, I probably would have considered getting in that line too.

Bob was completely surprised by the turnout and enthusiasm of the crowd at that parade in 1979.

> I never, ever could have envisioned anything like that. On the way back on the plane, our PR guy was handing out parade routes that we were going to go on and said, "There'll be cars to meet here and then we're gonna drive through the city, and we're gonna end up at Robson Square ..." I remember saying, "I hope there's people there because it would be a little embarrassing if there's not that many people there." Sure enough, we get off the plane, and you could feel it right at the airport. There were people at the airport to meet us. We drove downtown ... then we ended up at Robson Square, and it was beyond my wildest dreams that anything could ever

happen like that here. And the fact that I literally grew up a stone's throw away from Empire Stadium.

Bob occasionally received some backlash from local fans, presumably for being more handsome and better at soccer than them. Although he may not have been the most skilled player on the Whitecaps, a team that was stacked with some pretty impressive talent in the late 1970s, you could never have taken issue with his drive and commitment as a player. And through sheer determination, he was also able to be an offensive force at times. In 1978, he scored ten goals and had

John Craven of the Vancouver Whitecaps shares the
Soccer Bowl trophy with fans during the 1979 victory parade.
COURTESY OF THE BC SPORTS HALL OF FAME.

seventeen assists, becoming the second leading scorer on the team and eleventh in the whole league. Even when some fans may have had issues with him, there were also those who stood up for and believed in him. My cousin Mike has a friend named Doug who was an excellent athlete in East Vancouver and a legendary tough guy. When I mentioned to Bob that I knew Doug, he lit up. "Doug! I love Doug! When you're around for the length of time that I have been, you have your peaks and valleys. I'd often run into Doug, and if anybody ever said anything bad about me, he'd be the first guy to have my back. He's just a vintage east ender."

Today, neither Bob nor Lui lives in East Vancouver, but it has a special place in their hearts. They were formed by the experiences that living next to the PNE grounds offered, and they are more than happy to talk about those early days. Reflecting on it, Lui says:

> The truth is that the east end gave me a lot of joy between playing at Grandview Legion and winning a Sun Tournament of Champions with the guys and being at Notre Dame and being a part of three British Columbia Championships ... going to Simon Fraser and playing against some top-calibre college teams at Empire Stadium was pretty good. Then going to the Lions. It doesn't get much better than that for a kid growing up there.

As someone who can't remember a time when Bob Lenarduzzi and Lui Passaglia were not part of the Vancouver landscape, I just assume that everybody knows who they are. However, I was talking to my brother-in-law, Steve, at lunch one day at work. We were discussing who I should interview for this book, and I said that someone had suggested I "try to get a Lenarduzzi." We were sitting with some women in their thirties, who overheard what I said. One of them, my friend Carrie, asked me, intrigued, "Oooh, what's a Lenarduzzi?" We laughed, but it also made me a little sad to think that the names that are so integral to my idea of Vancouver are lost on people from a younger generation. I guess in the end, everything is temporary, and all our stories are as fleeting as the cheers that floated past Clelia Lenarduzzi on her porch that summer night in 1978.

Bob Lenarduzzi being congratulated by teammates after scoring a goal at Empire Stadium.
PHOTO BY KENT KALLBERG, COURTESY OF THE BC SPORTS HALL OF FAME.

CHAPTER 11

The Crump Twins

ON A RAINY VANCOUVER MORNING in mid-March, I brought my dad with me to interview Ronnie Crump, who was eighty-two at the time. They had worked together on the waterfront for thirty-five years, and it had been a while since my dad stopped by Ronnie's care home for a visit. He would occasionally go to visit with another longshoreman friend, Leo, who dropped by often to keep Ronnie company. Ronnie and his twin brother, Robert, made up the musical duo the Crump Twins, who performed for several years at the PNE Fair when they were young. One of the first things Ronnie excitedly shared with me is a memory of a daredevil. "Do you remember the guy that was shot over the wheel? He was shot over the Ferris wheel." Listening to him recount stories that took place on the fairgrounds and throughout the city, I was reminded that a story about the PNE is really a story about Vancouver. Ronnie and Robert are important threads in the fabric of the city. Their story weaves through jazz joints, boxing rings, exhibition stages, the waterfront, and beyond. They jammed onstage with Jimi Hendrix, were inducted into the

BC Entertainment Hall of Fame, and were the first Black men in Canada to be certified to operate a train.

Ronnie lives in a modest room with a bed, a chair, a nightstand, and a dresser with a TV on top. There are large pictures and posters of the Crump Twins on his walls. One shows the boys at about ten years old, dressed identically in plaid shirts and dark pants, standing in front of a shoeshine stand, shine cloths tucked into their belts. Another one features them as teenagers in matching red blazers and newsboy caps on the cover of *British Columbia Magazine*. There is a poster from when they performed at the Hollywood Bowl and a large photograph of Ronnie and Robert in their sixties, sporting matching goatees, with the caption "The Dream Team." A whole life in a handful of posters.

The Crump Twins dancing at the PNE.
COURTESY OF KAREN BERGLOV.

I asked Ronnie about his time performing at the PNE, and he said with a chuckle, "They had two shows. A Black show and a white show. You can guess which show we were on." He happily tells me about one-legged tap dancers, burlesque performers, and more. In 1950, at the age of eleven, Ronnie and Robert tap danced in a PNE show called Stars of Harlem, even though they were born in Alberta and lived in Vancouver. It was exciting for them to be onstage, but it wasn't the first time they performed on the PNE grounds. They had started their careers in entertainment a few years before, between bouts at boxing matches at the PNE Gardens. At eight years old, Robert and Ronnie would get into the ring wearing boxing gloves and shorts to spar in front of the cheering crowds. The boys would flip a coin before the "fight" to see who was going to take a dive and pretend to be knocked out. The approving crowd tossed change, which the boys would keep as their payment for the night.

The thrill the boys got from performing soon extended to tap dancing after their dad taught them some basic moves to get them started. Their father, originally from Oklahoma, worked as a porter for the Canadian Pacific Railway. He would often meet African American entertainers on the train when they came to perform in the city. On occasion, he invited them for dinner at the Crump home on Keefer Street, a couple of blocks from Hogan's Alley. Vancouver is the only major city in Canada without a Black neighbourhood, but it wasn't always that way. Hogan's Alley, located on the edge of Chinatown, was home to up to eight hundred Black residents at one point. However, the city had been eyeing the area for part of a potential freeway for years. A series of laws was enacted to intentionally keep the area "blighted" and poor. By the time it was appropriated and demolished to make way for the Georgia Viaduct, which opened in 1972, most of the Black residents had already dispersed throughout the city. The viaduct, which is essentially a bridge over land, was intended to be part of the freeway that was never built. In a spot that should have

The Crump Twins started their careers in show business boxing
between rounds of professional fights.
COURTESY OF KAREN BERGLOV.

been a bridge to the past, now stands the crumbling reminder of a failed plan. Luckily, there are a few people like Ronnie here to remind us of what stood there before.

The Crump Twins became a musical duo, with Robert on guitar and vocals and Ronnie on drums. "Robert was our lead man, but we harmonized," says Ronnie. They played throughout the city at places like the Cave and the New Delhi, where Jimi Hendrix would drop by to sit in with the twins. "His parents knew my parents and went to the same church." They also performed onstage with Louis Armstrong on three separate occasions.

When the twins performed at the PNE, they were part of an all-Black variety show. Ronnie is proud to have shared the stage with performers like LaWanda Page, an actress, comedian, dancer, and fire swallower who went on to be a mainstream star in the 1970s as part of the cast of *Sanford and Son*. Ronnie is still amazed when he talks about Henry "Crip" Heard, a one-legged, one-armed tap dancer from Memphis, Tennessee. Crip, short for the out-of-favour term *crippled*, earned his nickname after his car got hit by a train and he lost an arm and a leg. Determined to continue his career as a dancer, Crip learned to tap dance on one leg. Robert "Bumps" Blackwell, a musician who co-wrote and produced many of Little Richard's biggest hits, including "Good Golly, Miss Molly" and "Long Tall Sally," also performed in the variety show. And the twins, who were teenagers for most of their time at the PNE, appreciated the burlesque dancers who were part of the show. Surrounded by performers with names like Brown Sugar, Stella by Starlight, and Lottie the Body, the adolescent Crump Twins enjoyed the view backstage. "There was a lot going on back there. They get ready for the next show, and all she was wearing was a little star and a smile, saying hi to everyone," Ronnie says with a grin.

Over the years, the PNE has done a great job of featuring big names from around the world while also showcasing homegrown talent; this allowed the Crump Twins to be on the same bill as some of the top

The Crump Twins performed for several years at the PNE.
COURTESY OF KAREN BERGLOV.

African American performers of their time. This was a great confidence boost for the twins and connected them to an important time in North American history that predates the civil rights movement of the 1960s. The struggle for equality is often seen as an American experience, but Black people in Vancouver have also experienced a sense of disenfranchisement. When Ronnie talked about his experiences with racism as a Black person in Vancouver, his cheerful disposition quickly changed. "Yeah, longshoring. They wouldn't hire Black people," he told me. Things began to change in 1960, when the twins got a start on the docks. For a while, Ronnie and Robert were often overlooked when jobs were being assigned. Sometimes, being with a white friend would help. Ronnie recalled, "I'd be on the job right away if I was with your dad, but if I was on my own, they'd be 'sorry, sorry, sorry.'" In time, the twins were able to work their

Ronnie Crump (left) and my dad, March 2022.
PHOTO BY NICK MARINO.

way up and became certified to operate trains within the docks. They established themselves as the Dream Team. Their performing career ended shortly after they started longshoring because they were able to make "a little more bread."

From the time they were born, Ronnie and Robert Crump did everything together. They progressed through show business as boxers, dancers, and musicians before landing permanent work on the waterfront. As a surviving twin, it must be difficult for Ronnie, but he has also experienced things that most of us never will.

Not every entertainment choice the PNE has made over the years has been perfect, but they have evolved. There are no longer parades of little people or contests where kids get their freckles publicly counted, but local performers continue to have the opportunity to shine in front of a hometown audience. Despite a few giant missteps along the way, the PNE has shown it can produce a wide variety of shows that keep people coming back for more.

CHAPTER 12

The Waiting

IN THE SUMMER OF 1985, I had just graduated from high school and was working my last summer at the fair. Sitting in the bingo tent day after day for two weeks straight was pretty monotonous. One way to spice things up, however, was to keep on the lookout for some girl's crazy ex-boyfriend who was planning on coming to the fair to beat me up. A week earlier, I had met Lisa, a short girl with an asymmetrical haircut, when she approached me at bingo, being very flirty. I got her number, and a couple of days later we went to see *Back to the Future* at the Odeon theatre on Granville Street. We ended up clumsily making out on the edge of a construction site at Canada Place until she got a nosebleed and we had to stop. We planned to see each other again, but the phone call I got that night was not about our next date. Instead, she was calling to give me the heads-up that she had told her ex-boyfriend Todd that we had gone out, and now he was really angry. For some reason, she'd also let Todd know that I worked at the bingo tent, and he was coming to see me. The next day at work, I just sat there, watching and waiting. I had no idea what Todd looked like, so I assumed that every teenage male who walked within twenty feet of our tent was going to attack me. As I collected money and gave change for cards, I kept thinking to myself, How did it come to this?

As a twelve-year-old, when I'd first started working at the fair, all I really wanted was to be in high school. Hours of studying the photographs and handwritten comments in my brother's yearbook had helped me put together a fantasy of what high school was going to be like for me. Five years later, I'd have said it didn't really turn out the way I had planned. I'd never really factored in the school part of high school. And by the time I hit Grade 12, I was sick of it. It felt like the same thing every day. The teachers would assign homework that I didn't do, to be handed in at classes I didn't attend, which would be reflected on the report card I didn't show my dad. I treated high school the way a jazz musician approaches a solo—it was the assignments I *didn't* complete that defined me. Somehow, I still graduated. My final report in June of 1985 showed that I had missed forty-five days of school that year. I'd skipped seventy-one classes in the third term alone. For my eight classes I took, these were my third-term marks: two Cs, five Ds, and one E. I'm not sure what the point of an E grade is, because trust me, it functions exactly the same as an F. But school was never about grades for me. It was about everything social—friends and girlfriends. On those two fronts, I cannot complain. But, as I was sitting in the bingo tent, waiting to get sucker-punched, I knew that some of the decisions I had made in high school had led me to this point.

I'd had a girlfriend in grades 10 and 11 named Anita, and it was great. We got along well and had lots of laughs. I had pursued her for a few months before convincing her to go out with me. When she finally agreed, I wrote this in my journal:

> When I went out with other girls I didn't care about their feelings or anything, but I really care about Anita. I honestly hope that this time next year I'm still going out with her. I'm quite sure I'm not going to break up and I don't think she will.

Well, I was right about one thing. Anita didn't break up with me. Two years after I wrote this head-over-heels declaration of love, though, I called Anita and told her I wanted to take a break for the summer. She was offended and decided it would be better if we took a break forever. (And on a side note, I know that journal entry makes me sound like an asshole. Maybe I was. Either way, it is embarrassing to read.)

So, we broke up, and one night shortly after that, my friends and I ran into some drunk Catholic school girls at Central Park in Burnaby. I hit it off with a tall pretty girl named Caitlin, but I couldn't get her number before the police showed up and put the stumbling girls into the back of a squad car. Caitlin was yelling her number to me through the window of the police car, but I didn't have a way to write it down. In a moment that I now recognize as extreme white privilege, one of the officers let me borrow his pen and a piece of paper from his notebook. I walked away that night feeling pretty pleased with myself, happy that Anita and I had taken that break.

The pleased feeling wore off pretty quickly. Once Anita moved on to another guy and the tall Catholic girl lost interest in me, I suddenly regretted suggesting the break that became a breakup. I'd gotten the freedom I wanted but regretted the cost. I spent most of Grade 12 trying to convince Anita to give me one more chance, but she rightly refused. So, a little over a year after asking Anita for a break, there I was in the bingo tent, waiting to get beaten up by the nosebleeder's ex.

"What's the matter? You're so quiet today." It was Dion, a co-worker in the tent. He was one of those guys I'd always been drawn to, a guy who didn't seem to care about consequences. He was a big guy, over six feet, and was able to seem calm and menacing at the same time while also on the edge of laughter. We had some fun together at the tent, though I wouldn't say we were friends outside of work.

"Some girl's ex-boyfriend is supposedly coming here to beat me up," I told him.

"Seriously? Do you know him?"

"No. I've never met him."

"So, this guy doesn't even know what you look like?" he asked.

"I don't think so."

"Then don't worry about it, man," he said with a laugh. "I'll say that *I'm* Nick Marino and I'll beat the shit out of him."

"Really?" I asked, thinking he was kidding.

"Sure, why not? I'll kill him."

"Okay," I said, "thanks," not sure if this was real but hoping it was.

"A little excitement today, Nicky!" he said and slapped me on the shoulder. He walked back over to his section, sat down, looked over at me, and nodded. Maybe this plan would work, I tried to convince myself.

Although Dion's offer helped me to relax a bit, I was relieved to go on my break, where I could be anonymous among the fairgoers. I usually bought a hamburger or a piece of pizza and walked around the midway, where most of the teenage girls were. I walked by the arcade where Red was guarding the punching bag machine. I didn't feel like hanging around, so I kept moving. The sounds of the fair rang out. The screams from the roller coaster, the pounding of the mallets in the Whac-a-Mole game, the laughter and cries of little kids, the ticking of the flapper on the crown and anchor wheel, and an array of bells, whistles, and horns fought for space in my head. I ended up walking farther than usual that day, past the beer tent where the workers were pocketing money from the extra kegs they brought in, past the Prize Home where kids stood like hostages with their worn-out parents. I ended up near one of the entrances on Renfrew Street, where I saw my friend Dave selling PNE programs. "Win a house! Win a car!" he called out, a phrase that has sold a million dreams over the years. He knew about the crazy ex-boyfriend and asked if there were any updates. I told him about Dion's offer, and he laughed. We made plans to meet after our shifts, and I started the long walk back to the bingo tent, hoping for the summer to end so I could stop worrying about this psychopath who was after me.

I was only days away from starting at Langara College, which had somehow accepted me despite my horrendous report card. The walk back gave me some time to reflect on my life in high school. Perhaps the most surprising development for me in Grade 12 was that I started the year as school president. It would have been cool to end the year as president, but I was impeached in April of 1985. I had brought shame to my position and had to be removed after climbing on the school roof during class time with my friend Doug. A teacher had seen me and yelled, "Get your ass down here right now, Marino!" In response, I quickly pulled my ass out, mooned him, and then climbed down. Doug and I laughed about it and went to buy snacks at the gas station across the street, thinking it would be a funny story. By the time we came back, word had spread about what I had done, and lots of people were looking and laughing. I assumed they were laughing with me, not at me. I didn't realize it was serious until a teacher came up to me, smugly waved in my face, and said, "Bye!" as if I were going to get kicked out of school.

I didn't get expelled, but I was suspended and relieved of my presidential duties. The worst part was telling my dad that he had to come to the school to see the principal because I had skipped out, climbed onto the roof, and dropped my pants at a teacher. He was visibly disappointed, and I couldn't blame him. I didn't know it at the time, but what may have made things worse for my dad was the fact that my brother had been suspended for a very similar incident a few years before. I never got to be the star high school athlete my brother was, but at least we had this in common.

As part of my punishment, I had to write a letter of apology to the teacher, who was actively trying to get me kicked out. I resented it because I knew if it had been one of the guys he liked, he would have just laughed. (In retrospect, I realize he had to do something about it, but at the time, I felt like I was the victim.) We didn't like each other, though, and probably for good reason. He had told Anita to break up with me, which seemed to be beyond the scope of his teaching duties. He had told her that guys were like buses—"there is another one coming every fifteen minutes, and if you go downtown, they're all over the place." That was reason enough for me to dislike him, and I'm sure I gave him a million reasons to reciprocate while I was in his class. Basically, my friends and I were constantly trying to undermine any authority we could at school, and he was always in our sights. So, when it came to writing the letter, I made it as over the top and sarcastic as I could. I recently found the letter and was surprised to see that I was cocky enough put it on official Killarney Secondary School letterhead that I stole from the office. Here is what I wrote (keep I mind, we hated each other):

> Because of the unfortunate incident that took place on Tuesday, I feel an apology is in order. Although I realize my actions were both unacceptable and inexcusable, I am hoping you can accept this apology. The incident, contrary to your initial belief, was not a reaction to your request, but rather a matter of bad timing and poor judgment. I am not condoning the incident, but I feel I should give my best possible explanation. Like many students, I think of you as more of an older friend than a teacher. I also assumed for the moment you felt the same toward me. Because of my poor judgment, the incident put these barriers back up. Also, being the first day back from spring break, and a sunny one at that, one might say I was struck with spring fever. My body was filled with reckless courage, my morals had all but disappeared, and in one thoughtless moment I lost your respect for me. It is obvious, because of my actions, you will feel resentment

toward me. There is one thing though, that I hope you keep in mind. This resentment should be directed at only me. It should not be directed or associated with my friends or the student council. I hope the other teachers who might hear of this unfortunate incident through the faculty grapevine will also keep their resentment focused on the right source. Please take this apology as both acceptable and tasteful, two things I'm going to have to improve on in the future.

I didn't mean a single word I wrote in this apology, but it seemed to satisfy the principal, who passed it to my dad after reading it during our meeting in his office. I watched my dad read it, and he looked genuinely proud of my writing. It was probably the only piece of work I had shown him in a few years. He passed it back to the principal, looked at me, and said, "Good job." I didn't get the same reaction from the teacher, though. When I took it to his office, he read it, angrily threw it back at me, and yelled, "THIS IS BULLSHIT!" At least we could both agree on that.

I ended up writing a few similar apology letters for other kids that year. At one point, the same teacher came up to me and said, "Everyone knows that you are writing these letters for the other kids, Marino!" I took it as a point of pride that my writing style was distinct enough to be recognizable even when I didn't use my own name. Oddly, writing sarcastic apology letters to angry teachers was one of the only assignments I enjoyed in high school.

Unfortunately, a sarcastic apology was not going to be enough if the angry ex-boyfriend was waiting for me when I got back to the bingo tent. I slowly walked back, unconcerned with the fact I was already fifteen minutes late from my break. Even though I was a face among thousands, I felt vulnerable, exposed. I was wearing my Clash concert T-shirt from the show at the Coliseum the previous fall. Since that show, I'd proudly worn my shirt as much as possible, as part of my carefully manufactured personality. It said "Mohawk Revenge" on the front and "Freedom is more vital than a job" on the back. In one of several contradictions I lived, I didn't have a mohawk and was wearing the shirt at my job. I wondered if the shirt identified me at all. I worried that Lisa had told her ex-boyfriend what I looked like and that I loved the Clash. I made it back to our tent without being punched, noticed no one was waiting for me, and took my seat.

The boss looked at me, tapped his watch, and raised his eyebrows. I shrugged and put out my palms, gesturing that I'd made a mistake. He smiled and shook his head. Then, I felt it. A slap on my shoulder that made me jump. I turned around quickly, expecting to get hit. Someone stood above me, laughing as I tried to regain my composure. It was Dion. He slapped me again on the arm. "Little jumpy today, Nicky!" he laughed.

"I thought you were …"

"I know what you thought. Don't worry about it, man."

"What do you mean?"

"He came here during your break."

"Shit! Seriously?"

Dion laughed again. "It's over, buddy. I scared him off."

"What happened?"

"He asked who Nick was and I said *I* was."

"Then what?"

"Then I asked him if he had a fucking problem with that. I told him to get the fuck out of here before I kicked his ass in front of everybody."

"What did he do?"

"He stood there for a second, so I stood up and took a step toward him, and he just turned around and walked away. It was hilarious."

"Oh shit! Thanks. That's great. That's such a relief. Wow. Okay. That's great."

"No problem, buddy. I'd stay away from that girl, though. She's a psycho, stirring shit up."

"Oh, for sure. Thanks again."

Finally, I was able to settle back into and enjoy the monotony of handing out bingo cards. I was suddenly thankful for the washed-out, boring clientele of the tent. More angry grandparents and weird single guys, please! I sat in my wooden chair, relaxed for the first time since the phone call last night, and took a moment to *not* look at the teenage girls walking by the tent. I looked over at Dion, laughed and nodded. He smiled, threw his head back, and started laughing too.

My 1984 employee pass.
COURTESY OF NICK MARINO.

CHAPTER 13

Two Cities

IN 1942, during the Second World War, Hastings Park, or the PNE grounds, was split into two sides, separated by a chain-link and barbed wire fence that was two and a half metres (eight feet) high. On one side of the fence were thousands of incarcerated Japanese Canadians who had been forcibly removed from their homes. Families were separated. Some lived in horse stalls that were infested with maggots and caked in animal waste. There were ten showers for 1,500 women. The toilets didn't flush. Instead, an open trough of rushing water ran beneath the makeshift seats. Children who were sick with mumps were isolated in a windowless underground storage facility; the only light that reached them was through the opening of a coal chute. Conditions were grim, uncertain, and inhumane. And on the other side of the fence was an amusement park called Happyland that featured rides, midway games, and a dance hall. Local kids would meet with friends, go on dates, and work part-time jobs while ignoring the incarcerated thousands on the other side of the fence. The imprisoned Japanese Canadians could hear the screams from the Big Dipper, the splash of the boat on the Shoot the Chutes, and the music coming from the Happyland Dance Hall. They could only watch from behind barbed wire as white couples held hands, shared laughs, and ate candied apples. Tom I. Tagami, who was twenty-two at the time of his incarceration, shared this story about his time at Hastings Park:

> One Saturday evening, after we finished our work, I sat by the window looking across Hastings Park at a dance hall called Happyland. The dance hall was just on the other side of the fence, where people were allowed to come and go freely. I watched a lively bunch of young people about my age—Caucasians—dancing to the popular music of Glenn Miller, such as "In the Mood," "Moonlight Serenade," and other songs. It was such a contrast to the miserable living conditions we were experiencing inside Hastings Park. It really hit me how unfair it was, that even though we were Canadian born, just because we were a visible minority, we were held in a barbed wire enclosure under guard. I was saddened at the thought that I was as Canadian as they were, but I was completely segregated from them.[34]

The fact that anyone would ever consider putting an "internment" camp next to an amusement park would be laughable if it weren't so tragic. However, that is exactly what happened in Vancouver. And really, it was the result of years of indignities forced upon the Japanese Canadians by racist and opportunistic provincial and federal governments. (It should be noted that although *internment* was the language used for the incarceration of Japanese Canadians at the time, the term is incorrect as it traditionally refers to the confinement of non-citizens. *Incarceration* is the preferred and more accurate term.)

After the attack on Pearl Harbor in December 1941, Canada declared war on Japan, and within months ordered the forced removal and incarceration of all Japanese Canadians within an exclusion zone of 160 kilometres (100 miles) from the Pacific coast. In all, 22,000 innocent people were forced from their homes. Many of them passed

Up to 1,200 men at a time used the Forum, an ice rink,
as a dormitory during their incarceration, 1942.
CITY OF VANCOUVER ARCHIVES 180-3541.

through the Hastings Park Manning Pool. Utaye Shimasaki recalled his arrival there like this: "When we got to Hastings Park, a bus came with some Mounties, and some of them were holding whips like for training a lion. They must have thought someone was going to run."[35]

Japanese Canadians were held at Hastings Park for several weeks, often months, before being assigned to road camps, detention camps, or prisoner of war (POW) camps. Those who protested the separation of families or were deemed potential troublemakers were shipped off to a POW camp in Ontario, where they were watched by armed guards in towers and had to wear uniforms with giant targets on their backs in case they tried to escape. Some families were sent to prairie provinces to work on sugar beet farms and lived in deplorable conditions, often forced to sleep in repurposed chicken coops. The vast majority of the incarcerated were Canadian citizens born in this country, but they were treated as enemies until four years *after* the war had ended.

Canadians have been incorrectly led to believe that national security was the reason Japanese Canadians were forcibly removed from their homes and incarcerated. It was argued that they were sympathetic to the Japanese war effort and would help Japan attack the Canadian West Coast. However, both the Canadian military and the RCMP made it clear that Japanese Canadians did not pose a threat and should not be incarcerated. Major General Kenneth Stuart wrote at the time, "From the army point of view, I cannot see that the Japanese Canadians constitute the slightest menace to national security." Lieutenant General Maurice A. Pope said, "At no point during the war or before it had I worried about the presence of the Japanese, fellow citizens or otherwise, on the Pacific Coast."[36] The RCMP also assured the Canadian government that "internment" was unnecessary, but a contingent of anti-Asian BC politicians fought to disenfranchise and ultimately remove Japanese Canadians from the province. In fact, the worst offender of all, Liberal MP Ian Mackenzie, ran on the hateful campaign slogan "No Japs from the Rockies to the Seas."

Once the incarceration began at Hastings Park and the media reinforced the justification of their removal, Vancouverites were quick to turn on their former Japanese Canadian neighbours. Mae Oikawa recalled:

All these [Caucasian] people in the streetcars would stare at us while we were lined up. It was horrible ... I would never want to see any people, it doesn't matter their race, go through what we went through. We didn't throw a bomb at anyone. We didn't kill anyone. We were Canadians. We were born in Canada. I would never want to see this happen to any other people.[37]

Tom I. Tagami also talked about the indignities of being gawked at by the rest of the city:

> Whenever we strolled around on the Renfrew Street side, we were forever being stared at by hundreds of curious bystanders on the other side of the high wire fence. Some were sympathetic but most would jeer at us, as if to say, We're finally getting rid of you guys. At this moment, I thought of all the wild animals and monkeys in cages at Stanley Park being stared at by thousands of people and how they must feel, being caged up. At least they got free peanuts and food from the onlookers.[38]

British Columbia has had a long history of anti-Asian hatred and policy making. The Chinese head tax, which was introduced in 1885 to curb Chinese immigration, was equal to two years' pay just to enter the country. In 1907, there were anti-Asian riots in the streets of Vancouver that saw Japanese Canadians defending their neighbourhood for two days as angry white mobs destroyed businesses and burned the Japanese Language School to the ground. The Canadian government rewarded the white rioters by limiting Japanese immigration to four hundred labourers per year, then decreasing that number to 150. Voter suppression was also very real in Canada. Japanese Canadians, whether they were citizens or not, were not allowed to vote. And when the opportunity arrived to potentially rid the province of anyone of Japanese descent, there was no shortage of racists in power to jump at the opportunity. At the Conference on Japanese Problems held in Ottawa in 1942, the BC representatives were so callous in their views of Japanese Canadians that a diplomat present at the meeting later commented, "They spoke of the Japanese Canadians in a way that Nazis would have spoken about Jewish Canadians. When they spoke, I felt in that room the physical presence of evil."[39]

Evil prevailed as the BC contingent convinced Prime Minister William Lyon Mackenzie King to order the incarceration of Japanese Canadians under the guise of national security. In reality, Lieutenant General Pope said that the war afforded "a heaven-sent opportunity [for the anti-Asian contingent of BC] to rid themselves of the Japanese economic menace forever more." He also claimed of his experience at the conference, "I came away from that meeting feeling dirty all over."[40]

Although Japanese Canadians spent the bulk of their incarceration in ghost towns, road camps, and detention camps in the interior of the province, Hastings Park was used as a holding pen between March and September of 1942 until crude accommodations could be prepared. However, the degrading experience of being detained on the fairgrounds, often in full view of the angry public, left an unforgettable impression on many who passed through. Mary Kitagawa had this to say about her experience:

> I just want to tell you about what the impact of this Hastings Park experience did to us. First of all, when you are put into a barn to live, that signifies that whoever was in power thought of us as animals, and I think they thought that they could do this to us by labelling us in a certain way. You know, this is something that I can't forget and my brothers and sisters can't forget. When you think of internment, the first thing we think about is Hastings Park because it was so traumatic. That dehumanizing experience is something you can't forget.[41]

Dr. Henry Shimizu finds disturbing parallels to Nazi Germany when describing his experience at Hastings Park.

> Hastings Park was surrounded by a chain-link eight-foot fence. There were several gates, and there was train

access with tracks for exhibition cargo. It was an ideal manning depot and therefore used to round up all the Japanese people who lived outside Greater Vancouver. We could be herded into the park with little trouble, just like the Nazis were doing with people in Europe at that time—how ironic.[42]

In a letter written to her brother after visiting the Hastings Park accommodations, writer Muriel Kitagawa described the living conditions like this:

The whole place is impregnated with the smell of ancient manure and maggots. Every other day it is swept with dichloride of lime or something, but you can't disguise horse smell, cow smell, sheep, pigs, rabbits, and goats. And is it dusty! The toilets are just a sheet metal trough, and up until now they did not have partitions or seats. The women kicked, so they put up partitions and a terribly makeshift seat ... As for the bunks, they were the most tragic things there. Steel and wooden frames with a thin, lumpy straw tick, a bolster, and three army blankets ... no sheets unless you bring your own. These are the "homes" of the women I saw ... These bunks were hung with sheets and blankets and clothes of every hue and variety ... a tent of colours, age and cleanliness, all hung in a pathetic attempt at privacy ... An old, old lady was crying, saying she would rather have died than have come to such a place ...[43]

And while Japanese Canadians were forced to live in these conditions, on the other side of the fence, hundreds if not thousands of people were enjoying themselves at an amusement park. A *Vancouver Sun* article from March 1942 with the headline "Happyland Holds

Women and children lived in horse stalls during the incarceration of Japanese Canadians, 1942.
CITY OF VANCOUVER ARCHIVES 180-3540.

Dances as Usual" reassures readers that the amusement park will continue to operate alongside the incarcerated Japanese Canadians:

> Happyland Ballroom at Hastings Park will not be affected by the establishment of the Japanese Clearing Station in the central area of the exhibition grounds, the management of the Pacific Coast amusement company, owners of Happyland, announced today. Dancing will continue as usual, every Wednesday and Saturday throughout the spring and summer dancing seasons. Certain rumours and newspaper headlines (not the *Vancouver Sun*) have given the impression that the entire park is closed to the public. This is not true according to the Happyland Management.

The area surrounding the Happyland operations will be kept open to the public as in the past.[44]

Two months later, another article in the *Vancouver Sun* announces the opening of Happyland's rides and midway:

> Happyland Gayway, Vancouver's "Coney Island," and mecca for thousands of northwest amusement fans will be officially open for the summer season tonight. With seventeen modern rides and games of all description the Hastings Park playground presents a varied program of entertainment. All amusements will be in full swing every evening and Saturday afternoons. The popular dances in the spacious Evergreen Ballroom will continue every Wednesday and Saturday with a special dance tonight and a holiday dance on Monday.[45]

This announcement appeared over two months after the first Japanese Canadians were incarcerated at Hastings Park.

The local newspapers played a pivotal role in shaping the narrative of what was happening at Hastings Park. In a time before the ubiquity of television, newspapers were the authority that people trusted. Sadly, the information being shared about the conditions at Hastings Park was at best inaccurate and, more commonly, absolute lies. In a front-page article in the *Vancouver Sun* on April 6, 1942, the logistics of the Hastings Park Manning Pool were explained. The article describes how each person was assessed upon entering their incarceration:

> The pivot for this entire evacuation is Hastings Park. Every Japanese in the coastal areas must go through this clearing pool. One of the big jobs of the Commission is to "sort 'em out" ... So every man is examined and every woman and boy and girl. All are catalogued to be

disposed of later in the right place. This is the reason and the necessity for having a place like Hastings Park.

The article also implies that Japanese Canadians are looking forward to being detained there.

> Some passes were available to Japanese still living in their city homes to visit their countrymen in the park. Within two or three weeks these people from the city will take their turns. They looked over the huge dormitories with wistful faces, but certainly they saw nothing in prospect to shock or even disturb them. Hundreds of children played on the spacious lawns. It was a glorious day and Hastings Park stands in a magnificent setting.

Later, the same article reflects on the situation that the Japanese Canadian children are in and claims, without irony: "What a hellish thing war is, to put these innocent children in the predicament they find themselves in!"[46]

Two Japanese sayings were commonly repeated throughout incarceration to help people find the strength and motivation to continue. The first is "Shigata ga nai," which loosely translates to, "Nothing can be done about it, so let's make the best of it." The other is "Kodomo no tame ni," which means, "For the sake of the children." And that is how many Japanese Canadians dealt with their incarceration. They kept their heads down, worked hard, and tried to make the best of it. They put on brave faces. They sacrificed in the hope of providing a better life for their children. Of course, this is a generalization, but it is also the most commonly repeated story by family members.

Even after the war ended in 1945, Japanese Canadians were not allowed to return to the coast. They were given the choice to move east of the Rockies or to return to Japan, a country most had never seen. Either way, they were not welcome in British Columbia. And even

Japanese Canadian men stuffing mattresses with straw
during their incarceration at Hastings Park, 1942.
CITY OF VANCOUVER ARCHIVES 180-3537.

if they had been, returning home was impossible since the government had already sold their houses and all their possessions without their consent. Once the true price of detaining Japanese Canadians became clear, the government decided to sell all their homes and belongings to fund the incarceration. Houses were sold below market value, fishing boats were scooped up, and personal belongings were auctioned off. The government had promised to keep the homes and possessions of Japanese Canadians safe, but in 1943, the fire sale began. A typical auction post in the *Vancouver Sun* on December 1943 lists the following available to bid on:

> Consisting of lovely Chesterfield suite (like new), circulating heater, BT electric modern washing machine, Simmons beds, dressers cupboards, etc. And many tools

and useful sundries. Also farm implements ... and piles of everything else imaginable. Refreshment booths on the grounds starts at 11 and runs till 6:00 PM.[47]

The actual owners of these auction items probably never saw any profit from the sales. People bought the stuff for cheap, and the government used the money to finance the continued incarceration. Many Japanese Canadians were unaware that their properties and possessions were being sold until after it happened. If they received any money, the amount was well below what their belongings were worth. Forcibly detained and dispossessed, they essentially had to start over from scratch after the war. Japanese Canadians were not allowed to return to the coast until 1949.

Only one Japanese Canadian out of the 22,000 incarcerated was able to return to his own property. At the age of sixteen, Zennosuke Inouye arrived in Canada in 1910. He worked in coal mines and logging camps before enlisting to fight for Canada in World War I. He was actually refused the right to enlist in Vancouver because he was of Japanese descent, so he went to Calgary to sign up for the war effort. He fought at Vimy Ridge, where he suffered a chest wound. After he was discharged, he bought thirty-two hectares (seventy-nine acres) of land in Surrey, BC, through the Soldier Settlement Board. The land was rugged and filled with rocks, stumps, and trees, but Inouye worked hard to clear it and set up a strawberry farm. He lived and worked there until 1942, when he was forcibly incarcerated and his property was seized. When Inouye discovered that his property was among those being designated for returning veterans of World War II, he campaigned to have his property returned. How could they take the property of one veteran to give to another? After writing eighty letters to politicians and to his former commanding officer, Inouye was finally given his land back in 1949. The 22,000 other Japanese Canadians would have to wait another forty years for redress.

So, how does the PNE fit into all of this? The land in Hastings Park that the Japanese Canadians were incarcerated on had been appropriated by the federal government, so the PNE Board didn't have any choice in that. The decision to keep the Happyland Dance Hall and amusement park open, however, was presumably within the control of the PNE. They made a financial decision. And forty years later, when they were given the opportunity to make the smallest of gestures, they made the wrong choice then too. The *Hastings Park 1942* blog has this description of the PNE Board's embarrassing misstep when Parks Canada made a plaque in remembrance of the incarceration:

> In 1984, the internment was acknowledged as a significant national event by the Parks Canada Historic Sites and Monuments Board. Unfortunately, when the plaque was ready to be installed in 1987, the PNE rejected putting the monument onto the grounds.[48]

Forty-five years after Hastings Park was used to confine incarcerated Japanese Canadians, the PNE did not see the event as significant enough to be acknowledged with a plaque. The proposed plaque read:

> CITY OF VANCOUVER
> Japanese Internment
> Fear of a Japanese attack during World War II provoked a demand for the removal of all residents of Japanese origin from the coast. In 1942 evacuation was ordered and ultimately over 8,000 people passed through the livestock building before being moved east.[49]

In some ways, it is good that this plaque wasn't used, as the message is ultimately wrong. It clings to the idea that Japanese Canadians were a threat that had to be dealt with. It says *evacuation* when *forcible removal* is more accurate. And it doesn't mention that most of the incarcerated residents were Canadian citizens. Instead, it still paints them as the "other." Eventually, a more detailed plaque was erected, and the Momiji Gardens were opened on the grounds in 1993 to recognize the injustice of the incarceration. Having some sort of recognition of what happened to Japanese Canadians at Hastings Park is a good thing, but it's hard to feel that it is enough. Hundreds of thousands of people come through the park every year, and most of them will never encounter the Momiji Gardens. When I sought it out, I was surprised at how small and out of the way it is. The least that the PNE could do is to make a significant effort to recognize the injustice that happened in their park with visible and respectful monuments, plaques, and education opportunities throughout the park. Though it still feels like too little, this has improved in recent years, with informational plaques now at the four remaining buildings that were used during the incarceration. And in 2021, the PNE announced plans for a Japanese Canadian Interpretive Centre at Hastings Park, which will be created in partnership with the Japanese Canadian Hastings Park Committee. The forced removal, incarceration, and dispossession of Japanese Canadians is one of the most shameful chapters in our province's history. The PNE should do everything in its power to make people aware of what happened out of respect for the thousands of people who endured it.

I'd like to give the last word to Tom I. Tagami, who had this to say after hearing about the PNE's refusal to put up a plaque in 1987:

> The PNE Board refused to permit the erection of a plaque offered as a gift by the government of Canada commemorating the internment of Japanese Canadians during the Second World War on PNE grounds. What are your reasons for not wanting this plaque erected on PNE grounds? It might be embarrassing for the people of British Columbia, especially of Vancouver, for reminding them of the shoddy treatment of their fellow Canadians

in 1942. The Board of the PNE is attempting to suppress the facts of history, but it is an actual fact of history that took place on these very grounds which eight thousand evacuees, including myself, experienced by September 30, 1942. Most affected were the women, children, and sick people who had to live in the smelly Livestock Building throughout the hot summer months. A plaque erected here explaining what took place would be a reminder to the future generations of what could happen to any one of them at any given time.[50]

CHAPTER 14

Stella!

ON THE DAY that my great-grandfather was murdered, the headline in the newspaper was "Richest Italian in Vancouver Is Shot." My grandma was only four years old when a gunman shot her dad twice in the back and left him for dead. Angelo Teti never saw the face of the man who killed him on the day he was gunned down, but he had seen it many times before. In fact, Angelo was the godfather to three of his killer's children. Their friendship was over by the time Mario Montanero repeatedly threatened to kill Angelo in the weeks leading up to the murder. He followed through at a real estate office on Main Street on a September morning in 1914. Here is how it was described in the newspaper:

> Teti was standing with his back to the street door, three feet away, when Montanero appeared at the entrance. He did not say a word, but drawing a .38 caliber revolver took aim for an instant and fired. The bullet struck Teti in the small of the back and penetrated his kidney. As the man staggered and fell, Montanero shot again, the bullet lodging in the counter. Montanero turned and fled along Main Street with a revolver in his hand.[51]

The men in the office attempted to pursue Montanero, but he turned the pistol on them and ran away. However, he was quickly arrested by a nearby officer who had heard the gunshots. Montanero, who still had the smoking gun in his hand when he was apprehended, pointed at Angelo and said, "Yes, I shot him." At the police station, Montanero was enraged when he heard that Angelo was still alive. He told detective Joe Ricci that he had left the house that day with the intention of killing Angelo Teti. Within twenty-four hours, my great-grandfather succumbed to his injuries, and Montanero was charged with murder. Angelo's wife, my great-grandmother, was left to raise seven children on her own. She was swindled out of properties and deals by unscrupulous lawyers and partners who took advantage of her inability to speak English and her inexperience in business. The Teti family fortune was wiped out with two bullets and a grudge.

My great-grandparents, Angelo and Sabina Teti.
COURTESY OF PAULA MARCANATO.

My great-grandfather worked as a miner in British Columbia after moving from Abruzzo, Italy, in 1890. One day, he traded shifts with a friend, who was killed hours later in a terrible explosion. Angelo decided that his time underground was over, and he was ready to make his mark on the world. He bought a rooming house, invested in properties, became a money lender, and was reportedly part owner of the landmark Sylvia Hotel when it opened in 1913. Mario Montanero owed Angelo $2,300 on a mortgage but refused to pay, even though he was two years behind on his payments. He allegedly told Angelo, "I'll pay you in bullets!" My great-grandfather ignored the threats, and Montanero was driven into a murderous rage, convinced that Angelo was going to foreclose on the mortgage and take his property. Soon Angelo was dead, and Montanero was sentenced to hang.

When the judge asked Montanero how he pleaded, he replied, "Guilty," but was quickly corrected by his lawyer, who changed the plea to not guilty. The evidence was clear, however, and the defence's attempt at an insanity plea was disregarded. Montanero showed no emotion as the judge sentenced him to the gallows. However, on the day before the planned hanging, his sentence was commuted to life in prison. And then, six years later, Montanero hatched a plan with another murderer while they shared a room in the prison hospital ward. Together, they sawed through the bars on the window, put dummy figures in their beds, and fled from the prison under the cover of night. Their escape wasn't noticed until the next morning. Police believed that the two killers crossed the border into the United States. A year later, the other escapee was discovered running a grocery store in Seattle. Montanero was never heard from again. My family believes that Montanero eventually made his way to Alaska, where his son took yearly hunting trips.

Although both my great-grandfather and his killer were gone from the city, their relatives remained. And in the city's Italian community, it was inevitable that there would still be contact between the families.

My mom told me that she and her sister went to the same school as Montanero's grandson in a classic your-grandpa-killed-my-grandpa scenario. I always felt bad for my grandma, having lost her dad before she even started school. She is the only grandparent I remember, as my grandpa died when I was two and my dad's parents died before I was born. My grandma, Stella, who we called Nan, was an East Side girl through and through. She went to Strathcona Elementary during the First World War, ran restaurants with her husband, Tony, and ended up living on Pender Street, two blocks from the PNE. She was born on August 16, 1910—the exact day that the PNE was officially opened by Prime Minister Wilfrid Laurier.

I was the youngest of her six grandchildren and was always excited when she was around. Growing up, we used to see Nan a couple of times a week, and she would join us for family vacations in the summer. She was funny and warm and giving—everything you could want in a grandma. And, like many grandmas, she always gave us a little more than our parents wanted us to get. She would regularly bring me packs of hockey cards, American gum that oozed green liquid, and even twenty-dollar bills. When my mom was in the hospital having surgery, Nan stayed with us, and I remember my sister riding a skateboard on the hardwood floor in the living room. My mom would have killed her. Nan just told her to stop behaving like a "stupid ass," which made us laugh.

One thing Nan really loved to do was gamble. Whether it was bingo, slot machines, or poker with the family after Christmas dinner, Nan always wanted in. Some of the greatest moments of my childhood were spent watching adults loudly gamble and tease each other once the Christmas turkey was cleared from the table. The games started out calmly enough, but there was always a breaking point when things would get crazy. My Auntie Dolores, possibly the funniest person I've ever known, would jokingly provoke the other gamblers, especially when they were losing. It might sound cruel, but

Auntie Dolores and me at the fair in 1981.
COURTESY OF NICK MARINO.

these were people who had been friends since childhood and had grown up mocking each other. Everyone dished it out, and most of them could take it. Hundreds of dollars were changing hands, drinks were flowing, cigars were being smoked, angry glances were being exchanged between husbands and wives over lost bets. And there, in the middle of it all, was Nan, her tongue green from drinking crème de menthe, laughing and yelling with the rest of them.

Once I started to meet other people's grandmas, I noticed that Nan was different. She was more fun, more relatable. When I became an adult, I realized that what made her different was that she didn't put up barriers, didn't look down on the younger generation. She was just an East Van girl who also happened to be an old lady. I can remember going to see her on hot summer days when she was well into her eighties; she would be tanning on the patio in a sundress with cucumber slices on her eyes. She used to smother her arms and legs with baby oil to get a deeper tan. She rarely wore her eyeglasses because she said they made her "look old." Nan was the youngest old person I ever knew, and people loved her for it. She lived with my aunt and uncle, and when my cousins' friends came over, they just called her Nan. Her generosity knew no bounds, especially when she was force-feeding me more sandwiches than I could ever possibly want. She'd make me four or five grilled cheeses at a time, and if I didn't finish them, she'd act surprised. "Your brother ate six of them," she'd tell me.

Nan was generous with her gambling too. I remember being at the PNE with her when I was a child. She would place bets for me at games like the pea wheel, the crown and anchor, or the birthday game. If I won, she'd give me the cash to go off and play some games or go on a ride. And if I didn't win, she'd still give me money. She didn't like to waste her time trying to win stuffed animals at the kiddie games. "Those things are a goddamned rip-off," she'd tell me, pulling me toward the gambling tents. She could stand at the pea wheel for

My grandma loved gambling at tents like this one.
CITY OF VANCOUVER ARCHIVES 180-7372.

hours, it seemed, loudly tapping her plastic bead on the counter when her number came up. "Here you go, Nicky. Go get something to eat and meet me back here," she'd say, forcing some rolled-up winnings into my hand.

Nan's love of gambling extended to bingo too, except not in the tent where I worked. We didn't give cash prizes, just toys and lamps and other trinkets. Nan wanted to win money, so she went to bingo games that paid cash. Throughout the year, she would spend a couple of nights a week in church basements and bingo halls, waiting for the caller to say the number she needed for her big payday, though she never referred to him as "the caller." He was always "that son of a bitch" or "that goddamned bastard" or some similar put-down. It usually went something like this: "I needed G-59 for so long, but do you think that son of a bitch would call it? No, that goddamned bastard called G-58 and G-57, but not *my* number." Even as a kid,

I found it funny that she thought the caller had any choice in the numbers that came up, that she thought he actually had it in for her.

When Nan was in her eighties, she got a keychain that could swear. There were four buttons on it, and each played a different phrase, like "eat shit" or "fuck you." She loved pulling it out when we played cards. If someone got rummy and caught her with a mitt full of points, they were told to "eat shit" by her keychain. It added to the fun for us and seemed to ease the pain of losing for her. She kept it in her purse, and one day, when she was paying for groceries at Safeway, the "fuck you" button got jammed against something and kept loudly swearing. Nan furiously dug through her purse, trying to stop it as the confused cashier watched a sweet old lady's bag swear at her. Nan loved telling people, "The girl's face went white as a goddamned ghost when she heard it go off."

Nan's sense of humour is what I always think of first. She laughed hard and loudly, punctuated by the occasional uncontrollable snort. We were once at a restaurant with a forgetful waitress who had buck teeth. When she walked away, Nan said, "Christ, she could eat a cob of corn through a picket fence," and let out a raspy laugh, betraying her years of smoking. If there was ever a cranky old waitress, Nan would laughingly say that she had "a face like a can of worms." When I think of her now, she is always laughing. There was also a sadness in her that I rarely ever saw, but it was there. She lived as a widow for thirty-two years, and when my mom—her daughter—died, it was hard for her. But my aunt and uncle's house, where Nan lived after her husband died, was always so full of laughter, stories, teasing, and food that I didn't think there was room in it for sadness. It was literally my happy place, where I could listen to my cousins Ed and Mikey and their friends tell stories of hockey games and nightclubs and stags and girls. It was where I could laugh until I cried with my cousin Paula as we quoted Steve Martin and did voices and characters to crack each other up. It was where I often stayed when I worked at the PNE,

My grandma and me at a wedding in the early 1980s.
COURTESY OF MIKE MARINO.

sleeping on the couch overnight and taking the bus or walking to the fair in the morning. Their house was so full of life, so vibrant that I only ever needed to be a bystander. I rarely tried to insert myself into conversations, happy just to listen to the banter that seemed never to stop. I was intimidated by the pace of the conversation—it always seemed to be spinning too fast for me to jump on. Instead, I took it all in and went to school and repeated their jokes to my friends, pretending they were my own. And even though I knew it wasn't her house, as my Uncle Mike liked to remind us, I always thought of it as Nan's place.

I grew up on the East Side, but it was my experiences at Nan's place that really connected me to East Vancouver, along with the stories my dad has shared with me over the years; I feel a connection that goes back further than the day I was born. I feel like part of me was there when Angelo was shot, when Nan cursed the bingo callers, when my dad rode his bike to Blaine to buy tobacco, when my aunt lit a bag of shit on fire on her teacher's porch, when my cousins snuck into the Coliseum—all of it. I took in these stories so many times over the years that they became part of me. As the last one in my family to still live within Vancouver city limits, I feel lucky to be part of such a lively history. We may not have turned out to be one of the richest Italian families in the city, like my great-grandfather became in such a short time, but we have a history that makes me happy and proud and a little bit sad. And I don't think you can ask for much more than that from a family.

My family in Birch Bay, 1968.
COURTESY OF MIKE MARINO.

CHAPTER 15

Pac-Man!

IT WAS THE WINTER OF 1985. A ceiling fan in the lounge was turned up to high, and a bar stool was being dragged directly underneath it. Larry Pack stood on a chair, then stepped carefully onto the teetering stool. He slowly straightened up, his neck bent to avoid the whirring blades. A chant of "PAC-MAN! PAC-MAN!" erupted throughout the lounge as he carefully inched his head closer. I had heard the legend of Pac-Man plenty of times since I started working at the restaurant. Larry, the former assistant manager, loved to party after hours and, after a few drinks, he liked to stop the ceiling fan with his head. Several employees had been excited to see him when he popped in tonight after the game. As I watched his head nearing the fan, I felt a little sorry for him. Was this really how he wanted to be remembered? He seemed too old to need this kind of attention. He had to be close to thirty, which might as well have been fifty to my eighteen-year-old self. But here he was, about to humiliate himself for our benefit, like an elementary student who eats a worm to draw a crowd.

Larry tucked his chin down and led the crown of his head into the fan blades. The first few smacks threatened to knock him off his chair, but he steadied his footing and pushed through the fan with the determination of an Olympic weightlifter and the grace of a seasick toddler. It took about ten seconds for Pac-Man to bring the fan to a complete stop. He took several whacks to his bald spot before raising his fist in victory, to the cheers of the restaurant staff. Then he quickly lowered his head, jumped off the wobbly bar stool, and was handed a flaming sambuca shooter. The "PAC-MAN! PAC-MAN!" chant resumed as he downed the fiery shot. He didn't look proud so much as relieved to be done. It had been a busy night, with the Canucks playing the Montreal Canadiens at the Pacific Coliseum right across the street. The last customers had stumbled out around midnight, and the staff, both front and back of house, were sharing drinks in the lounge.

My first job outside of working at the PNE was at a restaurant called the Sirloiner, directly across the street from the fairgrounds. We depended heavily on events at the PNE grounds to drive customers to the restaurant. Our biggest nights were always when the Canucks played, bringing a mad rush of hockey fans wolfing down bitter Caesar salads, overcooked baked potatoes, and cheap cuts of steak. Every dish was garnished with a piece of raw kale to fill up the plate and make it look a little healthier. This was before anyone actually ate kale. As a busboy, I scraped the untouched leaves into the garbage. An assistant manager once bit into a piece of kale on a dare to show us that it really was edible. We all shuddered as if he had just swallowed a spider.

The racetrack at Hastings Park also created a lot of business for us, especially on weekends. The post-race crowd were big drinkers and often included several jockeys, who would sit in the lounge under the ceiling fan that made Pac-Man famous and get drunk. And loud. And sometimes, if one of them had enough to drink, he would do back-flips. This would unnerve the other customers and anger the cocktail waitresses. The manager would remind the jockeys to settle down, but it rarely made a difference. Even though most of them hovered around five feet tall, I found jockeys intimidating; there was an intensity in those wiry men that almost dared you to test them.

I didn't grow up close to Hastings Park, but the first ten years of my working life took place either at the PNE or right across the street from it. It was in those times when I was working less than a hundred feet from the fairgrounds that I noticed just how much of an impact the PNE had on the surrounding neighbourhood. In some cases, there were benefits: lots of foot traffic for nearby businesses, opportunities to rent out your backyard as a parking lot during events, and an unregulated playground for local kids. I spoke to writer Wayde Compton about growing up near the PNE, and he told me that his family house was actually on the property. "Our house was owned by the PNE. Mom and Dad paid rent to the PNE." His house was eventually demolished to make way for the Cassiar Connector, which removed one of the last remaining traffic lights on the Trans-Canada Highway. Wayde recalls making money from parking at an early age: "We had an empty lot right next to us. So as a little kid, I would hustle cars in that empty lot. We just filled it with as many cars as we could and made a fortune, me and my brother." Wayde also recalls the way he and his friends would sneak into Playland throughout the summer.

> Here's my scam at the PNE, and we used to do this every summer. We would get bolt cutters and cut a hole in the chain-link fence. If you cut it in a straight line, it would go back in position, and you couldn't tell it was open. We'd cut a hole at the beginning of the summer and just get into Playland every day. Eventually they'd find it, and one day you'd go and it would be all wired up. Yeah, we did that regularly.

For many adults, living next to the PNE wasn't as thrilling as it was for the kids. In 1973, Bob Williams, the MLA for Vancouver East, said, "Too often, the PNE is simply a burden on the people of the east side of the town. They have to live with the traffic problems almost daily as a result of that development. They have to deal daily with the mammoth invasion or intrusion into their residential neighborhoods. I know that can't be washed away, but it would be easier to take if the PNE were more responsive to their own needs right in the community."[52] Ten-year-old Wayde Compton may have been thrilled that he could listen to Cheap Trick through his bedroom window when they performed at Empire Stadium in the summer of 1983, but his neighbours possibly would have preferred some peace and quiet.

Traffic was the biggest inconvenience to the locals because there were so many events throughout the year. When the Canucks were playing at the Pacific Coliseum, they would play at least forty-five games a year, if you included the pre-season. And when they made the playoffs, they usually played two or three more. The BC Lions played approximately ten football games a year at Empire Stadium, and the Whitecaps played about twenty soccer games a season on the same pitch. Add in the seventeen days of the fair, concerts, satellite TV events, and boat shows, and there were easily more than a hundred nights a year when traffic would be a serious problem along the major corridors around the PNE. When thousands of people are converging on one area of the city at the same time, there isn't much that can be done. A few traffic cops at major intersections don't really make a difference. So, for about a third of the year, neighbours of the PNE would have to deal with gridlock before and after events. The only silver lining to all this traffic congestion was the opportunity to charge people to park on your property.

Not everyone wants to stand out on the street waving a piece of cardboard that says "PARKING" in hopes of squeezing another car onto their property, but there are always several grandmas willing to brave the weather to pocket a few dollars. Although many of these ladies are out hustling cars throughout the year, their most lucrative time is the PNE Fair in August. The sight of these parking ladies waving their signs on Renfrew Street is an indication of things to come. The same way that a robin announces the beginning of spring, or an army of Italians overreacting on Commercial Drive signals that the World Cup has arrived, grandmas flagging down motorists near Hastings and Renfrew remind us that there are only a couple more weeks of summer.

When I worked at the Sirloiner, I occasionally dealt with the parking ladies. If I was running late for work on the night of a Canucks game and didn't have time to park ten blocks away, I would give one of these ladies what amounted to an hour's pay to park my car. The exchange was done with minimal English and a lot of nodding and smiling before the cash transaction. Occasionally there were young people selling spots. I remember one twenty-year-old woman apologizing while she took my money, explaining that she needed it to go out clubbing. I paid her and walked to the restaurant to start my shift serving boisterous Canucks fans, who were often big drinkers and small tippers.

When I first started, I quickly learned that there is a definite hierarchy in a restaurant, with the manager at the top and the dishwasher at the bottom. Bartenders are above servers, and servers look down on bussers. Hosts are above bussers, but below servers. The kitchen staff generally hates the servers and often themselves too. But friendships cross levels, and most restaurant staffs are a big dysfunctional family. The Sirloiner on Renfrew Street in the mid-1980s was no different. Also, like with most families, if you look hard enough, there are probably a few people selling drugs. There were three competing weed dealers on staff at one point, with no lack of customers. It was a supply and demand thing. We probably could have used four.

At first, I was surprised at the number of employees who regularly worked while stoned. Soon, it seemed normal for about a third of the staff to be high while on shift. One night, one of the line cooks walked out of the kitchen in the middle of his shift, told the assistant manager that he was quitting, and went home. It caused a bit of a panic as it was the night of a Canucks game, and the restaurant was packed. We all wondered why he had quit, but the answer was quite simple. It turned out that he was too stoned to work, and the flames on the grill were freaking him out. He had mistakenly eaten too big of a piece of hash before work, and when it kicked in, he was unable to deal with the intensity of the kitchen. If he had been more responsible and eaten a reasonably sized piece of hash, I guess it could have been avoided.

My time at the restaurant was generally fun, though anyone who has worked in one knows it can be a high-stress job. When I became a waiter at nineteen, I rarely was treated respectfully by the tables of men guzzling Molson Canadians and shovelling in handfuls of nachos. They would have preferred to be waited on by the pretty female servers, who would endure a bit of flirting for a 10 percent tip. What these guys didn't hear was the way these women talked about them once they were out of the dining room. When I first started, I was shocked by the change in demeanour of the servers as soon as they stepped into the kitchen. The forced smiles and fake laughs they gave the customers quickly turned to anger and disdain a half step out of the dining room. In seconds it went from, "Oh, you are so funny! Let me check on those potato skins for you," to "If that troll at table 23 doesn't stop staring at my tits, I'm going to put a steak knife in his eye." Although I occasionally resented the pre-game crowds who swarmed the restaurant before the puck dropped across the street, I also understood their importance to the survival of the restaurant. If it weren't for the presence the tight-fisted, loud-mouthed hockey fans gorging themselves on bacon-wrapped scallops and zucchini sticks between swills of beer, I wouldn't have had a job. And once the Canucks moved to the new arena downtown, lots of East Van restaurant employees found themselves out of work.

So, while in a job that was almost completely dependent on my former employer, I realized that the PNE is bigger than the simple boundaries drawn on a city map. The PNE also includes the hockey fans who park on lawns and stumble through neighbourhoods, the howling concertgoers who guzzle warm cans of beer while pissing on backyard fences, and even the confused line cooks driven to unemployment by improper dosing. You can think of them as collateral damage or community outreach. Either way, the PNE, with all its events and traffic headaches, was the beast that anchored the east side of the city and set the tone for the area. Like the video game character Pac-Man himself, the unofficial representatives of the PNE travel through the surrounding neighbourhood, gobbling everything in their path. And like Larry Pack, the PNE would take several whacks to the back of the head over the years before landing on its feet once again.

CHAPTER 16

Empire

"The most disgusting exhibition of mass hysteria
and lunacy the city has ever witnessed."
—John Kirkwood, *Vancouver Sun*,
in a review of Elvis Presley in Vancouver[53]

THE LAST TIME ELVIS PRESLEY PERFORMED outside of the United States was at Empire Stadium on August 31, 1957. It was the first concert in the stadium, which had opened on the PNE grounds just three years before. Expectations were high among teenagers, especially girls, but the anti-Elvis sentiment among adults was just as strong. A headline on the front page of the *Vancouver Sun* from the day of the concert reads, "Daughter Wants to See Elvis? Kick Her in the Teeth." The writer had seen Elvis the night before in Spokane, Washington, and had written the article as a warning to parents. Here is his opening sentence: "It's hardly original, but if any daughter of mine broke out of the woodshed to see Elvis Presley in Empire Stadium, I'd kick her teeth in." It's an odd way to protect your own child, but I guess he'd rather have a toothless daughter than a horny one. He goes on to describe watching Elvis move his hips.

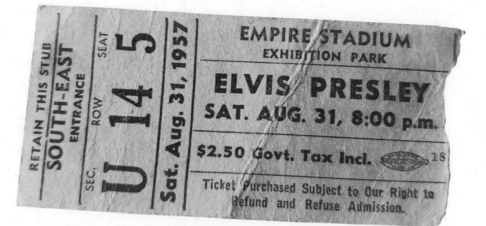

A ticket from the Elvis concert at Empire Stadium in 1957.
COURTESY OF ARTHUR AND DOREEN SADLER.

An aerial view of Empire Stadium during a BC Lions game.
CITY OF VANCOUVER ARCHIVES 180-3624.

His bumps and grinds, although odious coming from a man, were in themselves no more erotic than half-witted scribbles on a fence ... and when he did the most grotesque and imbecilic things with his body, they screamed and quivered, and shut their eyes, and reached out their hands to him as for salvation. It is a frightening thing for a man to watch his women debase themselves ...[54]

Parents in Vancouver were reading this article in the evening paper while their teenage sons and daughters were at Empire Stadium being corrupted by the King of Rock and Roll himself. And somewhere among the swooning and screaming throngs of girls was my mom, Diane, who was sixteen at the time, though I seriously cannot picture her losing it like some of the others. She kept her ticket stub from the show in a jewellery box, one of her prized possessions. I never saw my mom wear any jewellery other than her wedding ring, but she was always happy to open that box and show me her ticket.

The concert proved to be as crazy as everyone expected, though it started calmly. The stage was set up on the field, and all the concert-goers were in the stands, creating a huge distance between Elvis and his fans. To make it feel a bit more intimate, Elvis was driven around the track in a convertible before the show. When he hit the stage in a gold lamé jacket and black pants, the girls screamed so loudly that many people could only hear the drums. Early into the set, fans stormed the field and rushed the stage. They were met by police officers and volunteer cadets with locked arms, blocking the way. The cadets were trampled, and officers desperately tried to hold the crowd back. Local disc jockey Red Robinson came onstage and pleaded with the crowd to calm down and move back. Here is how one fan described what happened that day, on the *Elvis History Blog*:

Shortly after Elvis started singing, the crowd ran onto the field and charged the stage. We were all herded back into the stands under the threat of the concert being cancelled. Elvis started to sing again, and it did not take long for the stands to empty. Donna grabbed my hand and yelled, "Let's go, Billy!" We were amongst the first to the barrier in front of the stage. A big Vancouver city policeman in the last line of "defence" tried to push Donna back. He made the mistake of pushing her on her breast to which Donna responded by kicking him in the crotch. I remember running by him as he threw up, suspended over the barrier that he had been protecting. We made it to the stage just in time to hear Red Robinson announce that Elvis had left the stadium.[55]

Another concertgoer, Marion Guild, described a similar experience in a *Province* article from 2007 that celebrated the fiftieth anniversary of the show.

It was pandemonium. All around me were other kids and cops. Suddenly, I saw my shoe underneath the foot of a cop. I tried to get his attention, to no avail. The next thing I knew, I was biting the cop's arm. He moved, I got my shoe and ended up right in front of the stage, where I was mesmerized by the beautiful sight of Elvis.[56]

And just in case you are starting to feel sorry for the police for getting kicked in the balls and bitten by teenage girls, a commenter named Jean on the *Elvis History Blog* remembers it this way:

Yes, I was there at age sixteen and still can feel the excitement to be a part of the crowd. The cops went absolutely wild and were assaulting people with their sticks without any qualms as to whether or not any of the crowd deserved the whacks. Fortunately, no hits came close to

Elvis Presley onstage at Empire Stadium in 1957.
PHOTO BY ANTHONY BAZAN, COURTESY OF ROB AND BEN FRITH / NEPTOON RECORDS.

my group, and we all thought we had died and gone to heaven to be able to see Elvis ... Just the best!!!![57]

In the end, Elvis was onstage for twenty-two minutes and performed only four songs for the 25,898 paying customers. His manager was worried about the crowd and cut the show short. Elvis left the stage and hid in an alcove behind the curtains as his band kept playing. To create a diversion, he passed his gold jacket to a crew member, who ran off to a waiting car, chased by the crazed fans, who stampeded a *Vancouver Sun* photographer in the process.

News reports of the concert focused on the "riot," and neither major paper in Vancouver published a picture of Elvis himself. Instead, images of rampaging fans were featured. The *Vancouver Sun* headline on the front page of the paper read, "Presley Fans Demented," under a photo of kids rushing the stage. Reporter John Kirkwood described the scene this way:

> It was like watching a demented army swarm down the hillside to do battle in the plain when those frenzied teenagers stormed the field. Elvis and his music played a small part in the dizzy circus. The big show was provided by Vancouver teenagers, transformed into writhing, frenzied idiots of delight by the savage jungle beat music.[58]

First-hand accounts of the concert show that the kids had a great time. Teens were finally being recognized as a distinct demographic in the 1950s, and rock and roll was one of the first things created specifically for them. No longer did they have to listen to the same music as their parents. Rock and roll was kicking down the door, and the kids loved it as much as the parents hated it. The thrill of rushing onto the field and being part of the cultural revolution spearheaded by artists like Elvis was intoxicating. I have been to hundreds of shows in my life, but I'm sure I've never felt the same surge of excitement as the fans at Empire Stadium did that night.

There wasn't another rock concert at Empire Stadium for seven years, until the Beatles came to town in 1964. The parallels between the two shows are amazing, with gatecrashing stage rushes, pleas from Red Robinson to calm down, and a shortened setlist out of fear for the safety of the audience and the performers. Beatlemania was at its height in North America when the Fab Four visited Vancouver. There was so much excitement in the city that the Beatles spent the day of the show driving around, because it would have been unsafe for them to get out of their car. A radio station hired a Ringo look-alike to drive by a downtown hotel. His vehicle was mobbed so aggressively by Beatles fans that he was reduced to tears.

When the Beatles arrived onstage, they were greeted the same way Elvis had been seven years earlier. The audience of 20,621, the largest of their whole North American tour, shrieked and screamed so loudly that it was difficult to hear any of the music. The crowd could

A ticket from the Beatles concert in 1964.
PHOTO BY ANTHONY BAZAN, COURTESY OF ROB AND BEN FRITH / NEPTOON RECORDS.

PAUL McCARTNEY　　GEORGE HARRISON　　JOHN LENNON
RINGO STARR

THE BEATLES　compliments of　Dairy Queen

Mr. L. Toban - 1725 East Broadway, Vancouver, B.C.

A promotional photo given out at Dairy Queen before the Beatles played Empire Stadium.
PHOTO BY ANTHONY BAZAN, COURTESY OF ROB AND BEN FRITH / NEPTOON RECORDS.

not be controlled and kept surging to the front of the barrier, which was manned by a hundred police officers. Unlike the Elvis show, the Beatles concert had seating on the field, but most kids abandoned their seats to try to get closer to the band. When Red Robinson was told by the Beatles manager to go onstage and ask the crowd to settle down, John Lennon told him to "Get the fuck off the stage," before realizing what was happening. The Beatles played five minutes longer than Elvis, managing to squeeze out twenty-seven minutes of music before running to a waiting car and being whisked straight to the airport.

There were no serious injuries at the show, but 185 people were treated by medical staff. A 1964 article in *The Province* claims that "most were delirious and temporarily deranged with emotional exhaustion brought on by hysteria. Some had to be revived by oxygen. Five were taken to General Hospital and released after treatment for cuts and bruises."[59]

Once again, the adults of Vancouver seemed to be confused and angered by rock and roll's grip on their children. *The Province* newspaper published an article by a University of British Columbia psychologist who attempted to explain the effects of Beatlemania. Dr. J.E. Ryan explained, "The release of tensions is generally good, but there must be better ways than the Beatles provide. However, it is better they go wild over the Beatles than become juvenile delinquents or become mentally ill."[60]

There is footage of the show available online, and it certainly looks dangerous, with all the kids rushing the stage, but much of the blame should be placed on the promoters of the event. Clearly, they didn't have proper safety and security protocols in effect. The Beatles themselves, still in their days of wearing matching suits, didn't do anything to encourage the crowd to be unsafe. Fortunately, no one was seriously injured, and twenty thousand local Beatles fans had the night of their lives. Vancouver would have to wait another fourteen years before there was another concert at Empire Stadium.

Heart headlined the Summer Sunday concert on August 27, 1978, with opening acts Nick Gilder, Bob Welch, and the Little River Band. Forty-four thousand people packed the stadium on a day that threatened to rain but never did. The audience was boisterous and excited throughout the day, but Heart, led by sisters Ann and Nancy Wilson, was the only band to really take the crowd to the next level. They weren't Elvis or the Beatles, but the kids could hear their songs, and no one had to ask Red Robinson to come out and calm the audience down. The state of rock music had changed drastically since the Beatles visited Vancouver. Concerts were no longer part of a cultural revolution. Live shows were now a piece of the marketing cycle of the music industry. Kids still got excited, but there wasn't the sense that they were at the start of something new—especially not with the types of bands that performed at stadium shows in the summer. Heart would return to Empire Stadium once more for Summer Sunday in 1981. The biggest show of the summer concerts at the stadium, however, was when Supertramp played in 1979.

In the late 1970s, Supertramp was as ubiquitous on FM radio as Fleetwood Mac, Pink Floyd, or the Eagles. Canadians bought their records in massive numbers—more than anywhere else. Supertramp had two albums that were certified diamond in Canada, meaning they went ten-times platinum. So, when their tour took them to Empire Stadium on August 11, 1979, the crowd was psyched. It was the place to be for teens and twentysomething rock fans looking to take in some keyboard-driven soft rock, or, as reviewer Vaughn Palmer called it in the *Vancouver Sun,* "sophisticated '70s rock with a rippling beat."[61] Forty thousand tickets were scooped up immediately, and the band probably could have filled the stadium again had they scheduled another. I remember liking their music when I was in elementary school, but I've never had the urge to revisit it. It is the antithesis of

In 1978, Heart played for 44,000 fans at the first concert in
Empire Stadium since the Beatles played in 1964.
CITY OF VANCOUVER ARCHIVES 180-4203.

the punk rock that I was gravitating to in my teens. Their music did
not incite riots or cause anyone to lose their minds and scream. It was
catchy easy-listening music that sounded good to stoners. Unlike the
reports of mayhem in the paper after the Elvis and Beatles shows,
the review of the Supertramp show in the *Vancouver Sun* praised the
restraint of the audience and the band. The review started like this:

> Congratulations to Supertramp and fans. You both passed
> the audition. Saturday's sell-out show at Empire Stadium
> was an all-round success. Inside, it was a dazzling display
> of state-of-the-art rock that had been expected. Outside
> it caused little of the disturbance that last summer's
> Empire Stadium whoop-up engendered, which bodes
> well for future outdoor shows.[62]

The band played for over two hours, and among the fans were my cousin Ed and his friends. Ed remembers watching one person storming the stage in slow motion. When the kids had rushed Elvis and the Beatles, it was spontaneous, driven by the passion and excitement of youth, much like the music being played. But when this one fan made his way from the back of the field to the front of the stage at Supertramp, there was nothing spontaneous about it. Ed watched a guy in a wheelchair slowly progressing along the field, the people he encountered politely moving out of his way. Group after group of audience members parted to let him through. Everything was going well until his wheelchair was blocked by rows of cables from the sound booth that were impossible to wheel over. The cables stretched all the way across the field, with no way around. He sat in his wheelchair for a few minutes, contemplating his options. Finally, he stood up, lifted his chair above his head, and walked over the cables. Ed and his friends laughed from the stands as the con man sat back down and continued to wheel forward, unimpeded, all the way to the front of the stage.

Although most Vancouverites remember Empire Stadium as the home of the BC Lions, Vancouver Whitecaps, and the Summer Sunday concert series, it was built specifically for the British Empire and Commonwealth Games in 1954. This competition was a showcase of the finest athletes in the British Empire and Commonwealth, including countries like South Africa, Australia, and Pakistan. The most famous moment of the 1954 games became known as the Miracle Mile and featured the only two men at the time to have ever run a mile in under four minutes. England's Roger Bannister was the first to break the four-minute barrier but was soon bested by Australia's John Landy, who set the world record at a race in Finland a month later. When the two raced in Vancouver on August 7, 1954, it was the most anticipated event of the games. Landy explained his strategy for the race this way:

> I was going to run from the front, I was going to break
> the four-minute mile, and I was going to break my world
> record. It was very high-risk strategy, and I knew I only
> had a fifty-fifty chance of pulling it off, but that was what
> I believed I needed to do and that is how I believed the
> race should be run.[63]

Landy's plan almost paid off, but with ninety metres (three hundred feet) remaining, he glanced over his left shoulder to check on Bannister's position. At that exact moment, Bannister passed on Landy's right side and kept Landy at bay until crossing the finish line and collapsing into the arms of a track official. Landy crossed the line less than a second later, and the Miracle Mile became the first time that two runners had ever run a mile in less than four minutes in the same race.

The moment when Landy looked over his shoulder while being passed by Bannister was commemorated with a bronze statue, which was unveiled in 1967 before a BC Lions game and still stands on the PNE property today. Both Landy and Bannister attended the ceremony and took part in an official ribbon cutting. Whenever my family walked by the statue, my dad would often point out that Landy was beaten because he looked back at the wrong moment. The lesson of the statue seems to be to stay focused, believe in yourself, and don't look back. It perfectly captures the drama of sport, but I always felt sorry for Landy. He was the world record holder before and after the Miracle Mile, as Bannister's winning time was slower than Landy's record-setting time in Finland. But we don't get to choose how we are remembered, and in this case, John Landy is frozen in time, making a mistake. Landy himself saw it otherwise, however. He didn't believe that his backward glance cost him the race.

> It wasn't the reason at all. I ran the race the best I could on
> the day, and he was the better runner. In the last hundred
> metres the lactic acid had set in to such an extent that I

Roger Bannister (left) and John Landy in probably the
most famous photo ever taken at Empire Stadium, 1954.
CITY OF VANCOUVER ARCHIVES 180-3607.

could do nothing but maintain my pace, and he was able
to accelerate. I have no regrets about the way it was run. I
had a lot of respect for Roger, and he had a lot of respect
for me.[64]

So maybe there is more than one lesson in the statue. It could
be as simple as "you win some, you lose some" or "running is fun,

but sometimes your legs get tired." It doesn't have to be some grand idea. Personally, I'm glad that there are no statues of me capturing the countless mistakes I've made in my life. I'm not sure how inspiring it would be to see a statue of me withdrawing from a college course because I saw a girl in the class whom I'd embarrassed myself in front of five years before. Or does anyone really need to see a statue of me buying the first Smash Mouth album? It would be a humbling reminder for me, sure, but I don't know if it would teach a universal lesson.

I walked by the Miracle Mile statue every time we went to a Vancouver Whitecaps soccer game. We had season tickets in section Y, row 28, and I had seat 15. My dad was able to go into the empty stadium before buying the tickets to find seats with the best sightlines. At Empire Stadium there was always the chance your view would be blocked by the enormous metal pillars that held up the roof. If you didn't plan correctly, you could spend your time swaying back and forth like a bar stool drunk, trying to get a clear view. My dad chose a section on the 35-yard line at the south end of the stadium, facing west, with a great view of the field.

For a few years in the late 1970s, the Whitecaps were the darlings of the Vancouver sports scene. We had dynamic players like Kevin Hector, a sharpshooter who was the epitome of calm and poise, Trevor Whymark, with hair like Roger Daltrey and an uncanny ability to score with his head, and Willie Johnston, who once took a swig of beer from a fan's cup before curling in a corner kick that led to a goal. On defence: Bob Lenarduzzi, as well as John Craven and Roger Kenyon, two old school, no-nonsense centre-backs who weren't afraid to lay anyone out. And in goal, we had Phil "Lofty" Parkes, a big, imposing keeper who twice won goalie of the year and once held Giorgio Chinaglia of the New York Cosmos while John Craven punched him in the nose. Sitting on our CKNW seat cushions, doing the Oggy Oggy Oggy chant, yelling "WHITE!" at one side of

Tickets for the Vancouver Whitecaps vs. the New York Cosmos and the Seattle Sounders, 1979.
COURTESY OF NICK MARINO.

the stadium and hearing spectators yell back "CAPS!" from the other side, singing along to "White Is the Colour," jumping up and cheering after every goal—it was all so much fun. The joy that the Whitecaps of 1978 and 1979 brought me has never been matched by any other team. It was a great bonding time for our family, and I think fondly of sitting at Empire Stadium on a warm summer evening, with the sun setting behind the roller coaster, watching the Caps put away another opponent on the way to becoming Soccer Bowl Champions in 1979.

The BC Lions, of the Canadian Football League, played at Empire Stadium from 1954 until 1982. My experience of seeing the BC Lions was a lot different than going to see the Whitecaps with my family. I only ever went to one football game at Empire Stadium. It was a summer evening in 1981, when I was thirteen, and my cousin Ed brought me along with his friends to see the Lions. I don't really remember anything about the game because all the action was in the stands. Ed and his friends were nineteen at the time, and drinking was a big part of the experience for them. They'd sneak in mickeys of rum and rye, drinking them throughout the game. They were loud, funny, and quite a handful if they were sitting behind you. At one point, one of Ed's friends fell over trying to get back to his seat and was caught by the other guys, lifted up, and tossed into the row in front of us. There were a lot of angry looks and a few half-hearted apologies, but mostly laughter and more drinks. I did my regular thing when I was with Ed and his friends: watched quietly, laughed loudly, and felt a little bit scared.

When the game ended, a torrential downpour started, and no one was dressed for it. The walk home was at least forty minutes, and Ed seemed to be worried that I was going to get soaked, so he decided to get me a souvenir hat to help keep me dry. Unfortunately, he got caught trying to steal it from a box beside the merchandise stand and was grabbed by an angry man in a blazer. He grabbed Ed's coat with two hands, looked directly into his eyes, and said, "Get the fuck out of here, you punk. If I ever see you try to steal from here again, you'll be banned!" There were a few moments of silence as we walked away into the downpour before one of Ed's friends spoke up.

"Holy shit, Ed! That was the boss of the whole place!"

"That's hilarious, Ed! You got thrown out by the top guy!" They were right back to the boisterous, laughing drunks they had been two minutes before. I followed along, soaking wet, happy to be included, and proud that Ed had put himself in danger for me.

Ed and his friends eventually got season tickets at the south end of the stadium, under the scoreboard. It was one of the cheapest sections in the stadium, attracting groups of teens and some dads with their kids. Some of the guys would get pretty drunk by halftime, and one of them had a habit of spilling his beer on a dad in front of them. The dad was a good sport about it, as Ed and his buddies were generally friendly and harmless, but he also didn't want to be covered in beer every game. So, one hot summer day, he showed up with a plastic rain poncho. He put it on, turned around, and said, "All right guys. You're not gonna get me wet anymore. If this is what I have to wear, then I'll wear this every game." And he wore that poncho, rain or shine, while the guys behind him drank and spilled beer and cheered for the Lions. For years, they sat under that scoreboard, sometimes sneaking off to a little maintenance room under the clock to continue partying. Sitting in the end zone was a relatively inexpensive way to have a good time with your friends, but it certainly wasn't the cheapest way to see a BC Lions game. If you really wanted to see the game but were low on cash, there were always the Nalley's Chip Seats at the north end of the stadium. That's where things truly got crazy.

Patrick, a friend of my brother's, used to sell food at hockey and football games. He was one of the vendors, or Dueck boys, carrying trays up and down the stairs at the Pacific Coliseum and Empire Stadium. I asked him if he ever went into the Nalley's Chip Seats with his tray to sell to the kids in there. He said, "You could go in there, but you were taking your life in your hands. You'd always come out a few short … Kids were always trying to rip you off. You had these big bags of chips, and little hands would grab them and run like hell, and you'd be stuck. You couldn't chase them."

The Nalley's Chip Seats were in a fenced-off section with its own separate entrance, exit, and washrooms. If you showed up with a bag of Nalley's brand chips or bought one outside the stadium, you could get in for free—but you could not go to any other area in the stadium. According to Patrick, this deal "attracted every crazy from around the Lower Mainland. So it was all kids with maybe the odd dad. It was pretty rough in there." A chain-link fence separated the people in the Chip Seats from the rest of society. For some, it was a feral playground. For others, it was a very public escape challenge.

My friend Steve saw quite a few games in the Chip Seats as a teen. His dad would drop him and a couple of friends off with their bags of chips for entry before heading up to his own more civilized seat in the stands. It was challenging to watch the game from the Chip Seats because there weren't any bleachers, so kids would have to stand on benches and wait for the rest of the stadium to cheer to find out whether the Lions had completed a pass or gotten a first down. When I asked Lui Passaglia if he remembered the Chip Seats from when he played at Empire Stadium, he laughed and said he used to go there as a kid, back when it was called the Woodward's Quarterback Club. The membership card for that club stated on the back, "Members are expected to conduct themselves in an orderly manner at all times." I'm not sure if the Nalley's Chip Seats had the same rule, but if they did, it certainly wasn't enforced. When I asked Steve about security in the Chip Seat section, he said, "I don't remember there being any attendant or anyone in charge of the section stopping anyone from doing anything." There were ushers on the other side of the fence to make sure no one escaped, but no one I asked remembers anyone on the inside supervising the kids. Steve recalls one scary incident that happened to him. "I was with my sister, and someone lifted up my hat, put a lit firecracker on my head, and put my hat back on. My sister swatted the hat off my head, and the firecracker blew. It terrified me."

Steve was one of the few kids in the section who bothered trying to watch the game. Mostly it was a *Lord of the Flies* playground that often saw kids playing football games of their own. Steve remembers it this way:

> There would be way more kids playing football in behind the benches than really watching the game. It was kind of chaos football too. It looked like twenty-on-twenty kind of games. It felt like elementary-school-recess-style football games. It would start out as touch, then it would always turn into some sort of tackle and then some sort of fight. There would be games and then there would be a fight and then it would stop. And then after some time, the game would restart again with different people. It would start as touch and then turn into tackle, then turn into a fight. I remember that would happen often.

The only time that everyone in the Chip Seats was focused on the game was when a ball was kicked toward the section. Patrick recalls:

> If a field goal or convert was ever kicked and the ball went into the Chip Seats, there was a mad scramble and fight to get it. Even if you did get it, you were not going to keep it all game, because somebody was gonna take it. Your best bet was to go home right away if you got that ball.

Steve remembers trying to get the ball one time.

> I can remember once going in there [for a field goal] and running away from the ball, not toward it. It was just insanity if a ball went in there. There would be guys who looked like they were twenty in that section. They would always be the guy that ended up with the ball. They would just beat everybody up and take the ball away.

Red Scardillo, from the arcade, told me that his friends would grab the ball after a field goal and throw it to him where he waited outside the stadium.

When they weren't beating the shit out of each other, some of the kids made it a goal to break out of the Chip Seats and get into the rest of the stadium. From his vantage point, vending in the stadium, Patrick recalls seeing kids try to make a break for it.

> It was obviously nuts. They had about four ushers manning a big gate on each of the east and west sides. It was a swinging gate, and basically the kids were locked into the Chip Seats. They couldn't get out. So, what they would do is, they would charge the fence. You'd get like twenty kids in a battering ram knocking down the fence, and then they would all scramble down into the track and disappear up into the regular seats so they could watch the game like everybody else.

My brother's friend Bruce often tried to escape the Chip Seats when he went to games in the late '70s.

> [Someone] brought some wire cutters. He cut the fence, and because I was the smallest guy, I'd go first. And then I would make it bigger. And then we would say, We'll meet at some section. And then the security people would literally be chasing us around. Eight or so kids running out through this fence. We just ran into the regular stands to get better seats. We did that a few times. Sometimes they would repair it, and we'd have to cut it again. The goal was always to get out, and it was fun.

Steve remembers the coolest part of the Nalley's Chip section was that when the game ended, the gates would open, and the kids could go out on the field. Steve would walk across the field to meet up with his dad, often feeling a little envious of the kids who brought their own football so they could throw it around on the Astroturf. I remember being on the turf at Empire Stadium a couple of times as a kid. I was surprised at how hard the field was, completely unlike the grass fields we played soccer on in the city. It was like a green carpet on top of cement—not an ideal surface to be tackled onto, but that's what the BC Lions dealt with until they moved from the PNE grounds.

BC Place stadium was opened on June 19, 1983, on the edge of downtown Vancouver. Although it was only six kilometres (3.7 miles) away from Empire Stadium, the real distance was much greater. It was the beginning of the exodus of entertainment and sporting events from the east side of the city. The Vancouver Whitecaps, the BC Lions, and the Vancouver Canucks would all eventually move away from the PNE, and the opening of BC Place was when it all started. It's hard to argue with the superiority of BC Place as a stadium. At Empire Stadium, you sat on a hard bench with no back to lean against, and you were lucky if your section happened to be covered. Thousands of people got rained on during soccer and football games; the concourses were narrow and crowded; parking was an issue for fans and for the neighbourhood; and the field itself was in terrible shape. There was a push to build a new stadium on the PNE site, but the False Creek plan was chosen, and the lights slowly went out on what was once ground zero for sports and entertainment fans in Vancouver. At the time, it was really exciting to get a new stadium. I was at the first game, a sold-out contest between the Whitecaps and the Seattle Sounders, played in front of 60,342 paying fans. As we cheered the Whitecaps to a 2–1 win, I wonder if anyone was thinking about what we had lost. Did anyone care that the PNE and all it had to offer the city was slowly being disassembled? We had charged to the new stadium with the blind enthusiasm of the Elvis fans who stormed the field in 1957. Meanwhile, the developers and city planners were slowly wheeling through a crowd that politely moved aside to let them through.

CHAPTER 17

Go West

EXPO 86 IS THE DIVIDING LINE between the city we were and the city we are, and the PNE is on the other side of that line now. It has never regained its prominence as an important cultural hub in Vancouver, but it has also resisted calls for its demise. When it was announced in the 1990s that Playland and the fair at the PNE would be removed from Hastings Park, that the rides would be dismantled, the buildings flattened, and that nature would return, it felt like a done deal. No one expected that in 2023, the Coaster would still be terrifying people, that anyone would pay six dollars to play Whac-a-Mole, and that Playland would be spending $9 million on another roller coaster when it was all supposed to return to green space.

In 1889, the province granted the unceded land of the Musqueam, Squamish, and Tsleil-Waututh Nations that makes up Hastings Park to the City of Vancouver on the condition that it was "for the use, recreation, and enjoyment of the public." Over the years, the PNE added buildings, fairs, professional sports teams, and more, blurring the original intent of the park as a place to be enjoyed by everyone. Ticket prices and admission fees were clearly making the use of Hastings Park more exclusive. East Van resident Guy Faint has made it his life's mission to have the PNE grounds returned to parkland. In a research journey that took him as far back as the English common law judgments of the 1500s, Faint discovered that "you can't use a public park for profit or utility."[65] Through exhaustive lobbying and protest, Faint was instrumental in the ongoing saga of the greening of Hastings Park. Because of his hard work, The PNE grounds have been partially transformed back into a green space over the last couple of decades. Some people hoped the new park would attract families and groups of friends to get back to nature in their own neighbourhood. Other people worried that it would become a hangout for low-lifes and criminals. But now that the amusement park shares the property with a rejuvenated green space, maybe both visions can be true.

I guess it was inevitable that Vancouver would be lured by the promise of being included in a club with places like London, Paris, and New York. Some people saw it as an opportunity to make a lot of money. Others were excited about the prestige that would come with being allowed into the club. Like schoolkids longing to be accepted by the cool kids, many Vancouverites were enticed by the idea of becoming popular, of being desired. When Cheap Trick sang "I Want You to Want Me" at Empire Stadium in 1983, it might as well have been Vancouver singing it to the world. It reminds me of my friend Louise, who in Grade 7 enviously looked upon the girls in her class who already wore bras. When she watched the Grade 7 boys grab a classmate's bra strap from behind and pull it back so it would loudly snap against their skin, she thought, Why can't that be me? She pestered her mom about it until they wound up at a department store in the bra section. The woman from the store took one look at Louise and said, "What did you bring her here for? She's not ready." And so, Louise had to go back to school without a bra and watch the other girls get all the "attention." It's funny how quickly our need for popularity outweighs our need for dignity.

It's a little easier to give up dignity when it's not your own. The transition to world-class city also made Vancouver one of the most expensive places to live on Earth. As the price of a house increased out of reach for the majority of people who grew up in the city, so did the price of rent, which contributed to a housing crisis in our city that keeps getting worse. Vancouver's Downtown Eastside has consistently been among the poorest neighbourhoods in the country. In the last seven years alone, there have been almost ten thousand overdose deaths in the province, and most of them have been in Vancouver. So, when we look at the benefits of being world class, we also need to look at the cost. Have we sacrificed some of our own to be part of an exclusive club? And who actually benefits from being in that club? It all depends on what version of the city you allow yourself to see. There are as many versions of Vancouver as there are people who live in it.

At some point in my teens, I finally realized that other people were not just characters in my story, that each of them had their own perspective that was as valid as mine. It was like being shown how a magic trick works. In Vancouver, we don't always accept the validity of everyone else's perspective, though. From our racist past to our evergreen disdain of the poor and drug addicted, there are perspectives often excluded from our vision of the city. As we all live in the communities we can afford, we need to remember that some people don't have the luxury of looking away. They lack the means to protect themselves from the brutal reality of a city that seems to only want to keep moving forward, getting bigger, taller, more influential. But does progress always have to be economic? Could the *class* in world class be measured in acts of humanity? How much progress have we really made since Expo 86? In some ways, we have created a city that evokes the divided world of Hastings Park in 1942, where the privileged majority strolled through Happyland without a thought for the people on the other side of the fence.

My last day working at the PNE was September 2, 1985. Soon I would move on to bussing tables at the Sirloiner and dropping classes at a community college. A week after the fair closed, our boss from the bingo tent, Sam, organized a work party at an Italian restaurant on Renfrew Street, about ten blocks from the fair. We all ordered and were served alcoholic drinks, though most of us were underage. Fifteen of us sat at a long table with Sam at the head of it. We ordered pizzas, fettucine alfredos, and Long Island iced teas. I had a light-hearted argument with someone about whether Live Aid was better than Woodstock. We laughed and talked about our futures. Sam was teased about his loud polyester dress shirt. People flirted. There was a rumour that a couple slipped away from the group and had sex in some bushes around the corner from the restaurant. It was a great work party and a nice way to end my PNE career.

Near the end of the night, one of the girls was a little drunk and started walking around the table, massaging people's shoulders. Right at the moment when she put her hands on me, my cousin's friend Doug, whom Bob Lenarduzzi referred to as a "vintage east ender," walked into the restaurant. He saw the girl behind me and loudly said, "All right, Nicky!" Everyone from our table looked over to see who said that, and within seconds, their whole perception of me changed. Doug was a legend in East Van. He was a great soccer player, a funny guy, and tough as nails. Throughout my childhood, I heard countless stories from my cousins of Doug setting guys straight. He was a nice guy too, occasionally helping out at my soccer practices when I was younger.

Dion, who had saved me from the crazy ex-boyfriend a week before, looked at me, impressed, and asked, "How do you know him?"

"I've known him all my life," I replied, as if he were my friend and not my cousin's. There were raised eyebrows and nods all around. I had done nothing to deserve the respect I felt, but I gladly took it.

It was another one of the many connections to East Vancouver and the PNE that keep coming up in my life. When Red, the bouncer, stayed in a room above the arcade throughout the fair, his roommate

My dad with his godson, Mark, on his knee. Mark worked
as a bouncer at the arcade with Red Scardillo.
COURTESY OF MIKE MARINO.

was my second cousin, Mark. It was also Mark who Red had to
pull back into the roller coaster when they were riding without any
restraints. Joe Ricci, the cop who interrogated my great-grandfather's
killer on the day of the murder, is the father of my aunt's best friend.
I still see his grandson Joey at family events. And Tom I. Tagami, who
watched the white kids going to the Happyland Dance Hall from the

wrong side of the fence in 1942, is the father of my PE teacher from high school. All these connections are inevitable when your family has lived in a city for more than a hundred years. It's easy to ignore them, but it is also just as easy to accept them, to let yourself be part of the fabric of the city. I've always been suspicious of civic pride, but I do appreciate the roots and connections my family has made in Vancouver over the years.

And as Vancouver becomes both richer and poorer at the same time, the PNE just keeps on doing its thing, the same thing that it has been doing since the day my grandma was born in 1910. I have to admit that when I first started doing research for this book, I was biased. I thought the PNE was scamming people, from customers to employees. However, I've come to realize that the PNE was the one being scammed. I have consistently been told that the PNE is a fair employer. People go out of their way to tell me that the PNE was a great place to work. An hour after I interviewed Red Scardillo, he sent me a text that said, "The '80s were the best time at the PNE. I hope you write about all the good things about that time." And he is right, unless you were a kid in the 1970s or '60s—then those were the best times. And that's also why the PNE doesn't have to change. I've heard adults complain that the PNE is the same every year, but that's the point. Why change a winning formula? I've never heard a kid complain that the PNE is always the same.

When you go to the fair as a kid, the possibilities seem endless. There isn't enough time to ride all the rides, play all the games, eat all the food, and watch all the shows, so you do as much as your parents will allow. You cling to the possibility that you will win that giant stuffed animal, that you will get that second bag of donuts, that you will ride that roller coaster one more time. And when you are a teenager, the fair is still full of possibility. Will I meet someone? Was that girl on the swings looking at me? What can I get for free? Even adults are lured into the possibility that they may win a house or win a car. It doesn't matter that most of these things won't happen; the PNE has been selling the idea that they *might* happen for the last hundred years. And considering the way the PNE has shown it can survive, I assume it will still be selling possibility at Hastings Park a hundred years from now.

My daughters, Maya (left) and Sydney (right),
on the Scrambler and the children's roller coaster.
COURTESY OF JEANNE MARINO.

EPILOGUE

When my daughter Maya was five years old, she was a bit too short to go on some of the rides at Playland with her sister Sydney, who was seven. It was frustrating for both of them when Maya couldn't quite reach the "You must be this tall to ride" line. So, my wife, Jeanne, made lifts for Maya's shoes, and when the family returned to Playland the following week, Maya proudly and falsely stood just above the line. I couldn't help but laugh that all these years later, I was still finding ways to scam at the PNE.

If you are wondering what happened to an impeached school president with a horrendous attendance record and worse marks, you might be surprised to learn that I ended up becoming an elementary school teacher in East Vancouver.

And every June, when we are all getting sick of school, we pile into parent volunteers' cars and take the seven-minute drive to what the students have been looking forward to all year: our field trip to Playland at the PNE.

And every year, I hope that I don't end up in the car with the kid who throws up, because one of them always does.

ACKNOWLEDGMENTS

This book would not have been possible without the support and guidance of my family and friends both old and new. It was an honour to be asked by Charlie Demers to write this book. His support and feedback were essential. I have been a fan of his since the first time I saw him do stand-up at El Cocal on Commercial Drive. I am proud to call Charlie my friend and urge you to check out his books, albums, and live comedy. Thanks to Jennifer Van Evra, whose freelance writing course inspired me to write this book. When I suggested writing an article on teens working at the PNE in the 1980s, she said it would be a good idea for a book. Thank you, Jennifer. I would have never written this without your suggestion.

I am grateful to my friends Chris Gielty and Steve Scarrow for giving me feedback in the early stages of my first draft. Thanks to Fernando Torres for helping me get some interviews.

Thank you to Graham Clark, Kevin Chong, and Wayde Compton for your time and support.

Thank you to everyone at Arsenal Pulp Press: Brian Lam, Robert Ballantyne, Catharine Chen, Cynara Geissler, Jazmin Welch, Erin Chan, and Jesmine Cham. You've made this a very enjoyable process for me.

There were so many people who were eager to share their stories with me. Thank you to Dan Stefan, Santino Scardillo, Brian Gielty, Christine Weber Craik, Eric Koprowski, Bob Lenarduzzi, Lui Passaglia, Sal, Al Campbell, Gloria Macarenko, Louise Thomson, Rob Frith, John Ronning, Cliff Ronning (I somehow erased your interview and was too embarrassed to call back—sorry), Terri-Lyn Storey, Isaac

Messinger, Bruce Kagetsu, Tom Tagami, Erika West, Ronnie Crump, and Karen Berglov.

Thank you to Linda Kawamoto Reid from the Nikkei National Museum & Cultural Centre in Burnaby for answering my questions and teaching me about the experience of Japanese Canadians during incarceration. I really appreciate the time you gave to me.

As a teacher myself, I want to thank the teacher who inspired and supported me as a writer while I was a student at Killarney Secondary. Mr. Barry Kennedy brought joy to his work and to my life. I hope that some of my students will one day think of me the way I think of him. Sadly, Mr. Kennedy passed away in 2014, but I hope his family knows how influential he still is to me both as a teacher and a writer.

Thank you to Lindsay Siu for taking my photograph. I asked you to make me look four years younger and ten pounds lighter, and I think it worked.

Thank you to Ken Dickinson for the cool desk.

Thank you to Dion D. for pretending to be me so I didn't get beaten up at the bingo tent in 1985. That would have been embarrassing.

Thank you to all my colleagues at Nootka Elementary School for listening to me talk about this book for the last year. You did a great job of seeming interested.

Finally, I want to thank my family. Without you, this book would not exist. My cousins, Mikey, Ed, and Paula, have brought more joy into my life than they will ever know. My Auntie Dolores and Uncle Mike could not have been more supportive and generous. Their place truly felt like a second home to me. Nan showed me unconditional love and taught me that you never actually have to get old. Thank you to Clara for all the encouragement. My sister, Angela, and brother, Mike, have been so supportive during the writing of this book and throughout my whole life. I miss those Monopoly games we played, which Mike always won! I want to thank my mom for always believing in me when I was a kid. It made a difference. And a huge thank you to my dad, Mike Marino, for being such a great role model. You showed me the importance of being kind, open-minded, and optimistic. And thanks for all your stories too!

To my daughters, Sydney and Maya, thank you for the endless hours of laughs and fun we've had. I am so proud of the creative, responsible, and kind adults you have become. Thank you for encouraging and supporting me through all of this. And finally, thank you to my wonderful wife, Jeanne. You have been my biggest supporter and are always there to encourage me to believe in myself. You always made me feel like I could do this. I hope you know how important your support has been in this whole process.

NOTES

1   Lee Bacchus, "Hanging on with the heat-baggers," *Vancouver Sun*, June 26, 1982.

2   "Wood coaster poll 2019: Top 25 wood coasters," *ElloCoaster*.

3   "Arson charges dismissed," *The Province* (Vancouver), December 30, 1968.

4   David Breen and Kenneth Coates, *The Pacific National Exhibition: An Illustrated History* (Vancouver: University of British Columbia Press, 1982), 27.

5   "Giant Dipper is greatest thrill, claim," *Vancouver Daily Province*, May 11, 1928.

6   Tom Hawthorn, "Riding the beast," *Vancouver Sun*, August 31, 1985.

7   Gail Buente, "The wild world of the roller coaster," *The Province* (Vancouver), August 21, 1983.

8   Hastings Park Working Committee and Vancouver Park Board, *The Greening of Hastings Park: Restoration Program* (Vancouver: The Committee, 1996), 3.

9   Hastings Park Working Committee and Vancouver Park Board, *The Greening of Hastings Park*, 23.

10   Neale Adams, "The PNE: Come to the fair, the barkers cry, there's a candy apple spirit in the old wreck yet," *Vancouver Sun*, August 20, 1977.

11   Jeani Read, "Stayin' alive," *The Province* (Vancouver), August 21, 1980.

12   "Attendance slips at 'boring' PNE but fun changes in works," *The Province* (Vancouver), August 30, 1977.

13   Nels Hamilton, "Small boy's night at the fair: Gee it was fun! Even sleeping with horses," *Vancouver Sun*, August 23, 1957.

14   "PNE Gayway tops Canada for honesty: Police keep booths in line, says official as fraud charge fails," *Vancouver Sun*, August 29, 1951.

15   Bill Ryan, "Midway 'sits down' in protest at rules: PNE operators hit 'Sunday school' regulations," *Vancouver Sun*, August 25, 1950.

16   "Thugs fire shot at freak show boss," *Vancouver Sun*, August 29, 1957.

17   "Keeping beautiful is easy when you have a head start like Miss PNE," *The Province* (Vancouver), September 2, 1955.

18   "Penticton gives PNE queen who wants to be a nurse," *Vancouver Sun*, September 3, 1964.

19   "Tears of joy, Burnaby lass '57 Miss PNE," *The Province* (Vancouver), August 29, 1957.

20   "Miss PNE of 1978!" *The Province* (Vancouver), August 23, 1978.

21   Fred Curtin, "PNE's different: Fair-goers rate it tops," *The Province* (Vancouver), August 31, 1959.

22   Stuart Jeffries, "American freakshow: The extraordinary tale of Truevine's Muse brothers," *The Guardian*, March 15, 2017.

23 "Medicine puts paid to freaks," *The Province* (Vancouver), August 29, 1959.

24 Myrtle Meyer Eldred, "Your baby and mine: Helping the child to overcome his fear of persons with bodily imperfections," *Vancouver Sun*, September 18, 1940.

25 "Freckle Face Championships," *Vancouver Sun*, August 29, 1941.

26 "Fairgoers jump to horse," *Vancouver Daily Province*, August 24, 1951.

27 Eve Johnson, "Food at the fair," *Vancouver Sun*, August 28, 1996.

28 Alyn Edwards, "Termite Taxi owner a true blue original: Restaurateur's Chrysler Town & Country was legendary on the car show circuit," *Vancouver Sun*, December 27, 2019.

29 Peter McMartin. "Bill's famous name not so hunky-dory," *Vancouver Sun*, February 29, 1980.

30 "Hunky Bill decision reserved," *Vancouver Sun*, July 22, 1983.

31 "The Pirate Ship," *Pacific National Exhibition*.

32 "PNE crash prompts power check," *Vancouver Sun*, August 25, 1980.

33 Farhan Devji, "The man who bleeds blue and white: Looking back on the legendary career of Bob Lenarduzzi," *Whitecapsfc.com*, May 2, 2014.

34 Tom I. Tagami, "Tom I. Tagami," *Hastings Park 1942*.

35 Utaye Shimasaki, "Utaye Shimasaki," *Hastings Park 1942*.

36 Ann Gomer Sunahara, *The Politics of Racism: The Uprooting of Japanese Canadians During the Second World War* (Toronto: Lorimer, 1981), 18.

37 Mae Oikawa, "Mae Oikawa," *Hastings Park 1942*.

38 Tagami, "Tom I. Tagami."

39 James H. Marsh, "Japanese Canadian internment: Prisoners in their own country," *The Canadian Encyclopedia*, February 23, 2012.

40 Sunahara, *The Politics of Racism*, 28.

41 Mary Kitagawa, "Mary Kitagawa," *Hastings Park 1942*.

42 Henry Shimizu, "Dr Henry Shimizu," *Hastings Park 1942*.

43 Muriel Kitagawa, *This Is My Own: Letters to Wes & Other Writings on Japanese Canadians, 1941–1948*, ed. Roy Miki (Vancouver: Talonbooks, 1985).

44 "Happyland holds dances as usual," *Vancouver Sun*, March 25, 1942.

45 "Happyland fun begins tonight," *Vancouver Daily Province*, May 22, 1942.

46 "No chance of exhibition this year: Fair grounds ready to house 12,000 in midsummer peak," *Vancouver Sun*, April 6, 1942.

47 "Auction: Monster Japanese auction sale," *Vancouver Sun*, December 11, 1943.

48 "Momiji Gardens," *Hastings Park 1942*.

49 From the personal archives of Daniel Tokawa.

50 Tagami, "Tom I. Tagami."

51 "Shot in the back by former friend: Angelo Teti, wealthy Italian, likely to die as result of attack: Mario Montanero admits he shot man who held mortgage," *Vancouver Daily Province*, September 14, 1914.

52 David Breen and Kenneth Coates, *Vancouver's Fair: An Administrative and Political History of the Pacific National Exhibition* (Vancouver: University of British Columbia Press, 1982), 149–50.

53 John Kirkwood, "Presley fans demented," *Vancouver Sun*, September 3, 1957.

54 Mac Reynolds, "Daughter wants to see Elvis? Kick her in the teeth," *Vancouver Sun*, August 31, 1957.

55 "Canadians remember Elvis' 1957 show in Vancouver, B.C.," *Elvis History Blog*.

56 David Spaner, "Next thing I knew, I was biting the cop's arm," *The Province* (Vancouver), August 19, 2007.

57 "Canadians remember Elvis' 1957 show in Vancouver, B.C."

58 Kirkwood, "Presley fans demented."

59 Barry Johnson, "Hardy handful saves 16,000 from disaster," *The Province* (Vancouver), August 24, 1964.

60 J.E. Ryan, "Must be a better way: Beatles open valve releasing emotions," *The Province* (Vancouver), August 24, 1964.

61 Vaughn Palmer, "Supertramp dazzles crowd in sell-out show," *Vancouver Sun*, August 13, 1979.

62 Palmer, "Supertramp dazzles crowd in sell-out show."

63 Duncan Mackay, "Roger Bannister beats John Landy in the 'Miracle Mile' at Vancouver 1954," *Inside the Games*, April 11, 2018.

64 Mackay, "Roger Bannister beats John Landy in the 'Miracle Mile' at Vancouver 1954."

65 Terry Glavin, "Barer of Hastings Park fraud deserves credit," *Vancouver Sun*, September 25, 1991.

REFERENCES

Adams, Neale. "The PNE: Come to the fair, the barkers cry, there's a candy apple spirit in the old wreck yet." *Vancouver Sun*, August 20, 1977.

"Arson charges dismissed." *The Province* (Vancouver), December 30, 1968.

"Attendance slips at 'boring' PNE but fun changes in works." *The Province* (Vancouver), August 30, 1977.

"Auction: Monster Japanese auction sale." *Vancouver Sun*, December 11, 1943.

Austin, Edie. "Vancouver blows its top giving a wild welcome to victorious Whitecaps." *Vancouver Sun*, September 10, 1979.

Bacchus, Lee. "Hanging on with the heat-baggers." *Vancouver Sun*, June 26, 1982.

"B.C.'s prettiest girls start grind toward PNE crown for charm." *The Province* (Vancouver), August 29, 1955.

"Bid to scuttle Transpo called 'irresponsible.'" *Vancouver Sun*, June 7, 1980.

Billingsley, Jim. "PNE visitors will take last ride this weekend on landmark tower." *Vancouver Sun*, August 30, 1979.

"Blonde now enters PNE queen show: 10,000 cheer as Kingcrest girl selected." *Vancouver Sun*, August 31, 1959.

Bocking, Michael. "Fears of financial fiasco plague the party." *Vancouver Sun*, September 27, 1980.

Bocking, Michael. "Harcourt accused of hypocrisy in criticizing B.C. Place growth." *Vancouver Sun*, July 16, 1981.

Boyd, Denny. "Girls, you were all lovely." *Vancouver Sun*, August 27, 1983.

Boyd, Denny. "Now story can be told." *Vancouver Sun*, September 12, 1979.

Boyd, Denny. "Who mourns Callister Park? The wake certainly isn't a sellout." *Vancouver Sun*, February 9, 1971.

Braddock, John. "Richard moves in best of circles, but job has ups, downs." *The Province* (Vancouver), August 20, 1979.

Breen, David, and Kenneth Coates. *The Pacific National Exhibition: An Illustrated History*. Vancouver: University of British Columbia Press, 1982.

Breen, David, and Kenneth Coates. *Vancouver's Fair: An Administrative and Political History of the Pacific National Exhibition*. Vancouver: University of British Columbia Press, 1982.

Buente, Gail. "The wild world of the roller coaster." *The Province* (Vancouver), August 21, 1983.

"Canadians remember Elvis' 1957 show in Vancouver, B.C." *Elvis History Blog*, accessed June 5, 2022, http://www.elvis-history-blog.com/elvis-vancouver.html.

"Children like polio exhibit." *Vancouver Sun*, August 30, 1950.

Curtin, Fred. "PNE's different: Fair-goers rate it tops." *The Province* (Vancouver), August 31, 1959.

Dawson, Jim. "Bumps—a producer who ripped it up." *Los Angeles Times*, March 31, 1985.

Devji, Farhan. "The man who bleeds blue and white: Looking back on the legendary career of Bob Lenarduzzi." *Whitecapsfc.com*, May 2, 2014, https://www.whitecapsfc.com/news/man-who-bleeds-blue-and-white-looking-back-legendary-career-bob-lenarduzzi/.

Edwards, Alyn. "Callister Park demolition derbies—early auto recycling: Wildly popular: Events spelled the end of the road for thousands of Vancouver's derelict cars." *Vancouver Sun*, November 27, 2015.

Edwards, Alyn. "Termite taxi owner a true blue original: Restauranteur's Chrysler Town & Country was legendary on the car show circuit." *Vancouver Sun*, December 27, 2019.

Eldred, Myrtle Meyer. "Your baby and mine: Helping the child to overcome his fear of persons with bodily imperfections." *Vancouver Sun*, September 18, 1940.

"Fair of the century fairest of them all." *The Province* (Vancouver), August 16, 1958.

"Fairgoers jump to horse." *Vancouver Daily Province*, August 24, 1951.

Fralic, Shelley. "New Playland aims to be super midway." *Vancouver Sun*, August 14, 1980.

"Freckle Face Championships." *Vancouver Sun*, August 29, 1941.

"Free X-rays at fair for 10,000 persons." *Vancouver Sun*, August 24, 1954.

Garr, Allen. Untitled column. *The Province* (Vancouver), November 23, 1980.

Garr, Allen. Untitled column. *The Province* (Vancouver), November 27, 1980.

Gellatly, Clare. "Many odd characters in side shows at fair." *Vancouver Sun*, August 29, 1949.

"Giant Dipper is greatest thrill, claim." *Vancouver Daily Province*, May 11, 1928.

Glavin, Terry. "Barer of Hastings Park fraud deserves credit." *Vancouver Sun*, September 25, 1991.

Gnam, Jared. "Ten good reasons to see the 'Caps." *The Province* (Vancouver), May 15, 2012.

"'Half a man' dances like man and half." *Vancouver Sun*, August 1, 1952.

Hamilton, Nels. "Small boy's night at the fair: Gee it was fun! Even sleeping with horses." *Vancouver Sun*, August 23, 1957.

"Happyland fun begins tonight." *Vancouver Daily Province*, May 22, 1942.

"Happyland holds dances as usual." *Vancouver Sun*, March 25, 1942.

Harvey, Anne. "More than just a pretty face." *Vancouver Sun*, August 25, 1976.

Hastings Park Working Committee and Vancouver Park Board. *The Greening of Hastings Park: Restoration Program*. Vancouver: The Committee, 1996.

Hawthorn, Tom. "Glitz, glamour, and a new queen." *The Province* (Vancouver), August 19, 1990.

Hawthorn, Tom. "Riding the beast." *Vancouver Sun*, August 31, 1985.

Hellman, Claire. "Sponge lady for a day." *Vancouver Sun*, August 15, 1992.

"He's down but not out." *Vancouver Sun*, August 31, 1951.

"Hunky Bill decision reserved." *Vancouver Sun*, July 22, 1983.

Jamieson, Jim. "Here's a star most modest." *The Province* (Vancouver), July 16, 1989.

Jeffries, Stuart. "American freakshow: The extraordinary tale of Truevine's Muse brothers." *The Guardian*, March 15, 2017. https://www.theguardian.com/books/2017/mar/15/american-freakshow-the-extraordinary-tale-of-ruevines-use-brothers.

Johnson, Barry. "Hardy handful saves 16,000 from disaster." *The Province* (Vancouver), August 24, 1964.

Johnson, Eve. "Food at the fair." *Vancouver Sun*, August 28, 1996.

Kearney, Jim. "Whitecaps could be start of something great." *Vancouver Sun*, September 10, 1979.

"Keeping beautiful is easy when you have a head start like Miss PNE." *The Province* (Vancouver), September 2, 1955.

Kirkwood, John. "Presley fans demented." *Vancouver Sun*, September 3, 1957.

Kitagawa, Mary. "Mary Kitagawa." *Hastings Park 1942*, accessed June 3, 2022, http://hastingspark1942.ca/hastings-park-stories/mary-kitagawa/.

Kitagawa, Muriel. *This Is My Own: Letters to Wes & Other Writings on Japanese Canadians, 1941–1948*, ed. Roy Miki. Vancouver: Talonbooks, 1985.

Krangle, Karen, and Michael Bocking. "Harcourt: Report card on Vancouver's mayor." *Vancouver Sun*, December 9, 1981.

"The look of a winner." *The Province* (Vancouver), August 20, 1980.

Mackay, Duncan. "Roger Bannister beats John Landy in the 'Miracle Mile' at Vancouver 1954." *Inside the Games*, April 11, 2018, https://www.insidethegames.biz/articles/106 3797/1-roger-bannister-beats-john-landy-in-the-miracle-mile-at-vancouver-1954.

Mackie, John. "Elvis, the Beatles and the Hayrick Rubes: The PNE has had a bit of everything over 100 years, including Happyland and the tattooed lady." *Vancouver Sun*, August 28, 2010.

Mackie, John. "One of Vancouver's most vibrant and notorious neighbourhoods gets the stamp of approval." *Vancouver Sun*, February 8, 2014.

Mackie, John. "Perogy king 'Hunky' Bill Konyk dead at 88: Winnipeg import sold his perogies at the fair for 52 years." *Vancouver Sun*, August 14, 2019.

Macy, Beth. *Truevine: Two Brothers, a Kidnapping, and a Mother's Quest: A True Story of the Jim Crow South*. New York: Little, Brown and Company, 2016.

"Man dies trying to get free Playland ride." *Vancouver Sun*, June 17, 1985.

Marsh, James H. "Japanese Canadian internment: Prisoners in their own country." *The Canadian Encyclopedia*, February 23, 2012, https://www.thecanadianencyclopedia .ca/en/article/japanese-internment-banished-and-beyond-tears-feature.

McIntyre, Gordon. "Squid-ink corn dogs, pho tacos among fun food available at PNE." *Vancouver Sun*, August 25, 2022.

McMartin, Peter. "Bill's famous name not so hunky-dory." *Vancouver Sun*, February 29, 1980.

McMartin, Peter. "Hero of the fair sets world mark on roller coaster." *Vancouver Sun*, August 27, 1979.

"Medicine puts paid to freaks." *The Province* (Vancouver), August 29, 1959.

"Midgets, fat lady arrive here Sunday." *Vancouver Sun*, August 23, 1941.

"Miss PNE of 1978!" *The Province* (Vancouver), August 23, 1978.

"Momiji Gardens." *Hastings Park 1942*, accessed June 5, 2022, http://hastingspark1942 .ca/history/momiji-gardens/.

Moore, Kerry. "A crown and banner VIP." *The Province* (Vancouver), August 27, 1989.

Mötley Crüe, with Neil Strauss. *The Dirt: Confessions of the World's Most Notorious Rock Band*. New York: HarperCollins, 2002.

"New Miss PNE: Winner has a poetic view of the world." *Vancouver Sun*, August 23, 1978.

Nichols, Marjorie. "'New' NPA stalks COPE turf." *Vancouver Sun*, November 30, 1985.

"No chance of exhibition this year: Fair grounds ready to house 12,000 in midsummer peak." *Vancouver Sun*, April 6, 1942.

Oikawa, Mae. "Mae Oikawa." *Hastings Park 1942*, accessed June 3, 2022, http://hastings park1942.ca/hastings-park-stories/mae-oikawa/.

"Outdoor life's the thing, says 17-year-old Miss PNE." *Vancouver Sun*, August 31, 1967.

Palmer, Vaughn. "Supertramp dazzles crowd in sell-out show." *Vancouver Sun*, August 13, 1979.

Pap, Elliot. "McKay roasted in *Post* article." *Vancouver Sun*, July 16, 1982.

"Penticton gives PNE queen who wants to be a nurse." *Vancouver Sun*, September 3, 1964.

"The Pirate Ship." *Pacific National Exhibition*, accessed November 10, 2022, https://www.pne.ca/rides/the-pirate-ship/.

"PNE crash prompts power check." *Vancouver Sun*, August 25, 1980.

"PNE Gayway tops Canada for honesty: Police keep booths in line, says official as fraud charge fails." *Vancouver Sun*, August 29, 1951.

"PNE's 66th season offers more than celebrity milking." *Globe and Mail*, August 21, 1981.

Read, Jeani. "Stayin' alive." *The Province* (Vancouver), August 21, 1980.

"Resurgence puts Black artists in mural fest spotlight." *Vancouver Sun*, July 20, 2021.

Reynolds, Mac. "Daughter wants to see Elvis? Kick her in the teeth." *Vancouver Sun*, August 31, 1957.

"Richest Italian in Vancouver Is Shot." *Victoria Daily Times*, September 22, 1914.

Ryan, Bill. "Midway 'sits down' in protest at rules: PNE operators hit 'Sunday school' regulations." *Vancouver Sun*, August 25, 1950.

Ryan, J.E. "Must be a better way: Beatles open valve releasing emotions." *The Province* (Vancouver), August 24, 1964.

Shimasaki, Utaye. "Utaye Shimasaki." *Hastings Park 1942*, accessed June 3, 2022, http://hastingspark1942.ca/hastings-park-stories/utaye-shimasaki/.

Shimizu, Henry. "Dr Henry Shimizu." *Hastings Park 1942*, accessed June 3, 2022, http://hastingspark1942.ca/hastings-park-stories/dr-henry-shimizu/.

"Shot in the back by former friend: Angelo Teti, wealthy Italian, likely to die as result of attack: Mario Montanero admits he shot man who held mortgage." *Vancouver Daily Province*, September 14, 1914.

Spaner, David. "Next thing I knew, I was biting the cop's arm." *The Province* (Vancouver), August 19, 2007.

"Stamp corsage's feature Spencer's war aid party." *Vancouver Sun*, August 12, 1942.

Stinson, Dan. "Lenarduzzis maintain the quiet life." *Vancouver Sun*, Saturday January 5, 1980.

"Stunting boy killed in fall from Giant Dipper: Loses balance while standing on head during ride." *Vancouver Sun*, September 2, 1938.

Sunahara, Ann Gomer. *The Politics of Racism: The Uprooting of Japanese Canadians During the Second World War*. Toronto: Lorimer, 1981.

Tagami, Tom I. "Tom I. Tagami." *Hastings Park 1942*, accessed May 29, 2022, http://hastingspark1942.ca/hastings-park-stories/tom-i-tagami/.

Taylor, Jim. "Effect of Callister decision haunts city." *The Province* (Vancouver), August 21, 1984.

Taylor, Jim. "Putting the hum back in bugged: Jolly season triggers a change in soft-hearted Jim Taylor that brings on the Humbug Awards." *The Province* (Vancouver), December 24, 1979.

"Tears of joy, Burnaby lass '57 Miss PNE." *The Province* (Vancouver), August 29, 1957.

"Thief grabs $80 from PNE show: Youth escapes in midway crowds; Children's Day sets new record." *Vancouver Sun*, August 29, 1950.

"This we saw…" *Vancouver Daily Province*, August 19, 1950.

"Thugs fire shot at freak show boss." *Vancouver Sun*, August 29, 1957.

Tucker, Cam. "This day in history: September 8, 1979." *Vancouver Sun*, September 8, 2012.

"20 racehorses perish in fire." *Vancouver Sun*, May 28, 1969.

"Valley girl PNE queen: Fort Langley winner wore a home-made dress." *Vancouver Sun*, August 30, 1956.

Wasserman, Jack. Untitled column. *Vancouver Sun*, August 26, 1959.

Wellens, Geoff. "Hats off to Mrs. Lenarduzzi." *The Province* (Vancouver), August 4, 1978.

"Whitecaps fever reigns." *Victoria Times*, September 10, 1979.

"Wood coaster poll 2019: Top 25 wood coasters." *ElloCoaster*, accessed September 13, 2022, https://www.ellocoaster.com/wood-results-2019/.

"Youths sought as suspects in $300,000 Playland fire." *Vancouver Sun*, September 10, 1968.

INDEX

Photo credit: Lindsay Siu

NICK MARINO is a writer and teacher from Vancouver. His family has lived in Vancouver for over a century and has deep roots in the East Side. Nick has performed at Just for Laughs Northwest, curated a series of comedy and music shows called Bite of the Underground, and taught comedy classes at Arts Umbrella. This is his first book.

East Side Story: Growing Up at the PNE is the latest title to be published under the Robin's Egg Books imprint. Robin's Egg Books features some of the freshest, smartest, and, above all, funniest writing on a variety of culturally relevant subjects. Titles in the imprint are curated and edited by comedian, playwright, and author Charles Demers.

Previous Robin's Egg Books:

Float like a Butterfly, Drink Mint Tea:
How I Beat the Shit Out of All My Addictions
by Alex Wood

So You're a Little Sad, So What? Nice Things to
Say to Yourself on Bad Days and Other Essays
by Alicia Tobin

What I Think Happened: An Underresearched
History of the Western World
by Evany Rosen

You Suck, Sir: Chronicles of a High School English
Teacher and the Smartass Students Who Schooled Him
by Paul Bae